Siberian Miracle

Peter de Bruijne is a freelance writer and graphic designer based in Holland. Previously he was Communications Dirctor at Open Doors for eleven years.

This is his first book.

Peter O. de Bruijne

Siberian Miracle

Translated by
Adrian Peetoom

MarshallPickering
An Imprint of HarperCollins*Publishers*

Marshall Pickering
An imprint of HarperCollins*Religious*
Part of HarperCollins*Publishers*
77–85 Fulham Palace Road
Hammersmith
London W6 8JB

First published in Dutch by Gideon in 1990
under the title *Louter Vuur*
First published in Great Britain by
Marshall Pickering 1991

Translation by Adrian Peetoom,
107 Parkwood Drive, Chatham,
Ontario N7M 2B1, Canada

A catalogue record for this book is
available from the British Library

ISBN 0 551 02579 4

Typeset by Medcalf Type Ltd, Bicester, Oxon
Printed and bound in Great Britain by
HarperCollinsManufacturing, Glasgow

Contents

Foreword

For every change
> someone,
> somewhere,
> *must* have paid a price.

I knew it all the time and everyone who has read the Bible knew it – and my guess is that everyone who knows himself knows it – there's got to be a price tag for changes in the right direction.

Change?

Only *one* illustration: years ago my colleague and I drove our rather big vehicle all the way to Moscow – every imaginable space filled with Bibles (maybe even every *un*-imaginable space). With the help of a Baptist pastor we determined the exact place where he would unpack and transfer the precious cargo to a vehicle he was to hire. We chose a place in the very shadow of the Kremlin – not as an act of defiance, but somehow figuring out that control would be less as one got closer to 'Headquarters'. It worked – but my! the prayers – the sweat – the tension.

And just imagine: we were back there recently, at approximately the same spot, only now right in front of Lenin's Mausoleum. Next to me a famous Russian evangelist – we talked, we preached and we gave out New Testaments! One man reached back to me with his New Testament and said: 'Could you write your name and address in it?' I did and after a while we went somewhere else.

But that's not the end. Last week I received a letter from somewhere in Russia, very touching. From a man who received a New Testament from me and 'you wrote your address and initials in it. Unfortunately we could not decipher your first name, but I think it says: Brother Andrew. Now we ask you urgently, if it is possible send us more literature and if at all possible: a Bible.'

What made the change? To a very large degree a relatively small group of people who defied the KGB and bravely proclaimed the Lordship of Jesus Christ. That's what this book is about and I want to warn and predict: you may not be able to put it down, so gripping is the story, so well written.

And I also predict that if God can find men and women like those in this book, He could use them to finish the Great Commission. Unless you think we need no change in the world today – in that case, all that is necessary for evil to conquer is for good people to do nothing.

'God wake us up through this book and take us where you want us.'

Brother Andrew

Introduction

Not so long ago Chuguyevka was just an obscure town in East Siberia. However, a small group of Christians transformed it into a symbol of Christian courage in the face of the blind hatred of the Soviet authorities towards the Church. The Chuguyevka Christians were not new to that hatred – they had know it since birth. Some had not known their own fathers, victims of the firing squad. But these martyred fathers stood as examples of Christians who had not been afraid, and served to remind the survivors to think about what the Bible has to say about fear, about love, and about the way a congregation has to function.

I would expect many readers to become enthusiastic admirers of the approach to life and the lifestyle of the young men and women in this book, and their 'experiment of unity'. But I'm sure that few would want to take on the consequences of similar decisions for themselves.

This book describes historical events, and I have used real names of friends and enemies. Before I wrote the first word, I had countless conversations with participants. Through careful notes and comparisons of eye witness stories a reliable account emerged.

Yet this is not a neat chronology, for I have deliberately chosen a thematic approach. The themes may not always be named specifically, but they will always focus on the task, the functioning and the struggles of the Church. I decided that comprehension would best be served through a number of personal stories, chosen to illustrate the working of the Church, and also of its opposition.

I could write a book about each member of the Chuguyevka congregation. Each one belongs in a parade of Soviet citizens we should admire, because they loved freedom above security. Together, they form a unique example of unity and perseverance, which perhaps is only comparable to the house churches in the Republic of China. It is my ardent prayer that their example finds emulation in my own church and in the worldwide Church of Jesus Christ.

Peter de Bruijne
Ermelo, The Netherlands

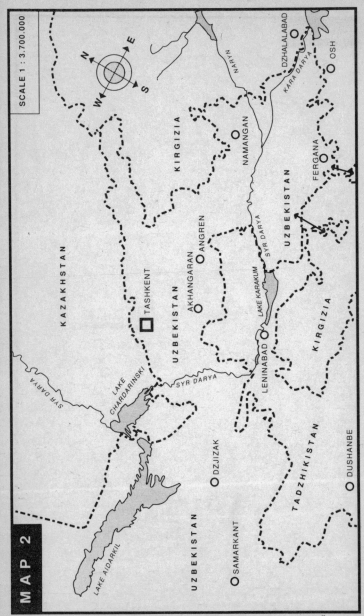

SCALE 1 : 3.700.000

MAP 2

COPYRIGHT PETER DE BRUIJNE · ERMELO · HOLLAND

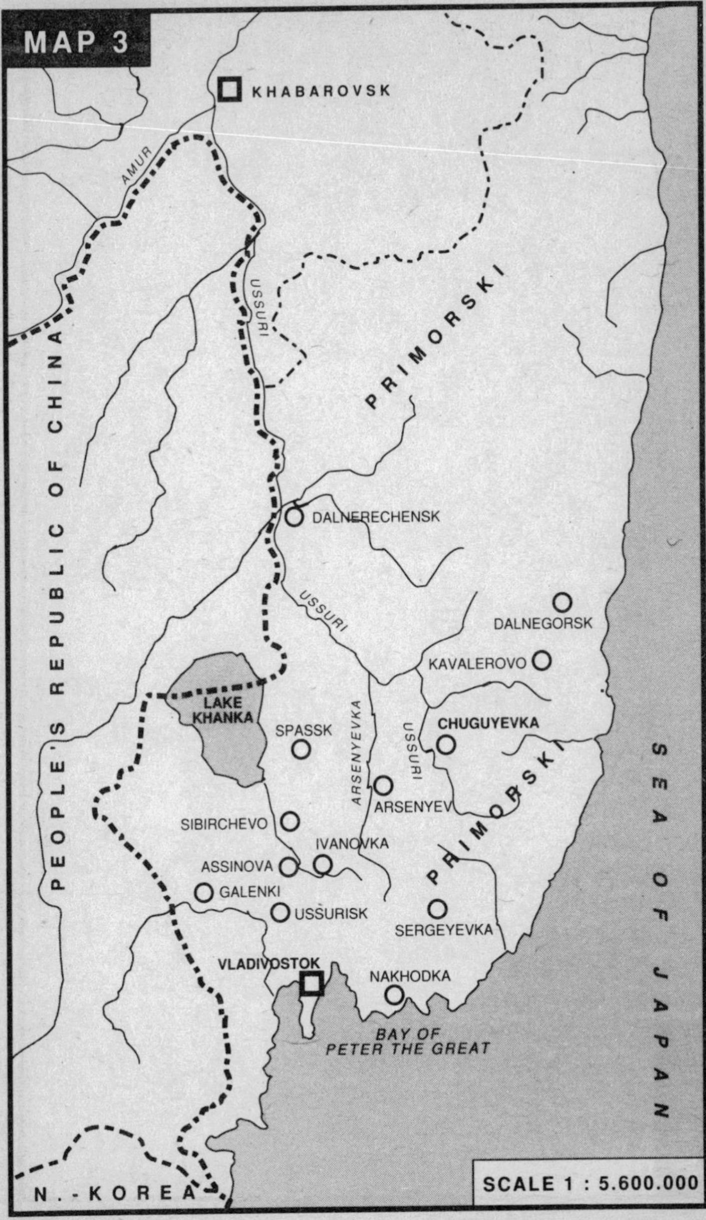

MAP 3

KHABAROVSK

PEOPLE'S REPUBLIC OF CHINA

PRIMORSKI

AMUR

USSURI

DALNERECHENSK

USSURI

DALNEGORSK

KAVALEROVO

LAKE KHANKA

ARSENYEVKA

CHUGUYEVKA

SPASSK

USSURI

PRIMORSKI

ARSENYEV

SIBIRCHEVO

IVANOVKA

ASSINOVA

GALENKI

USSURISK

SERGEYEVKA

VLADIVOSTOK

NAKHODKA

BAY OF PETER THE GREAT

SEA OF JAPAN

N.-KOREA

COPYRIGHT PETER DE BRUIJNE - ERMELO - HOLLAND

SCALE 1 : 5.600.000

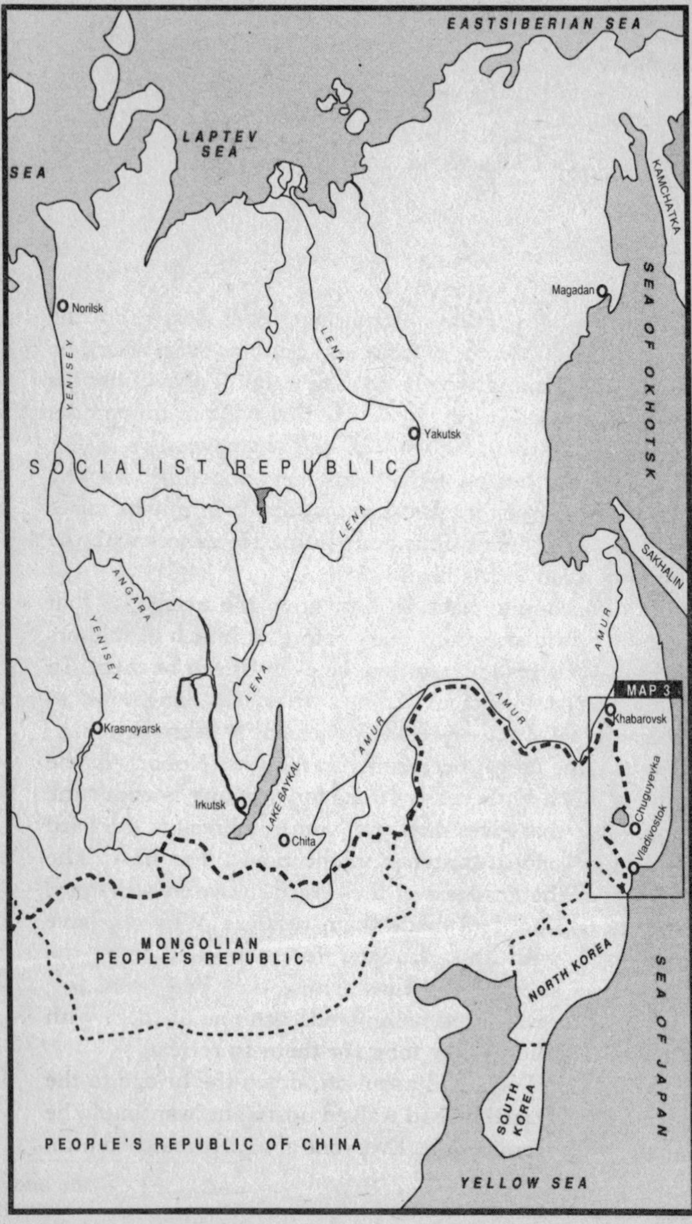

EASTSIBERIAN SEA

LAPTEV SEA

SEA

KAMCHATKA

Norilsk

Magadan

SEA OF OKHOTSK

YENISEY

LENA

Yakutsk

SOCIALIST REPUBLIC

LENA

SAKHALIN

ANGARA

YENISEY

AMUR

LENA

AMUR

MAP 3

Krasnoyarsk

AMUR

Khabarovsk

LAKE BAYKAL

Irkutsk

Chuguyevka

Chita

Vladivostok

MONGOLIAN PEOPLE'S REPUBLIC

NORTH KOREA

SEA OF JAPAN

SOUTH KOREA

PEOPLE'S REPUBLIC OF CHINA

YELLOW SEA

1
The River

Chuguyevka, 25th August 1980

Bright sunlight reflects off the white pebbles. From the right, the left, from in front and behind, everywhere he hears the sound of swiftly flowing water. Tolya blinks his eyes. Slowly he begins to realize that he is in the middle of the Ussuri river. He's still alive! Tolya Sheludkov hasn't drowned but lies on a riverbank surrounded by swirling waters. A sharp stone sticks in his ribs. Painfully he raises himself. Every part of his body hurts. He winces with the blinding pain in his head.

It's all coming back to him now, the events of that afternoon and also from years before. A bunch of soldiers stood on the bridge, ten, maybe even fifteen of them. In Chuguyevka everybody knows that it's dangerous to challenge Tolya, especially when he's been drinking. Actually, he hasn't been sober in months. Nobody in the area is much bothered by that, for drinking is about the only thing that gives men and women a break in the hard and monotonous existence in the Soviet Far East. The soldiers on that bridge over the Ussuri river were also tipsy, and the alcohol had made them reckless. Why not have some fun with this drunken forest worker from the Sokolovka suburb? But how wrong they had been, for, drunk as he was, he'd hammered each one of them with his fists. It didn't take long for them to retreat.

Still wild, Tolya had taken off, down the bridge to the river bank. Dazed he had walked upstream, wanting to be alone, away from people. Everyone always threatened him.

He hated them all. He hated himself too. Only the wilds brought him peace. Only in the far-flung forests, the taiga, did he feel at home. He had never been afraid of the wild animals which populate this most eastern province of the Soviet Union. He had faced bears, wolves and other predators, but he had never been afraid.

Tolya grows dizzy and drops his head on his arms. When he closes his eyes the jabs of pain stop. Now he remembers how he had fallen into the Ussuri river, half-unconscious already. The cold water had revived him a bit, but the strong current had already taken him down quite a distance. He had thrashed in the water, lost his breath and had felt himself sucked to the bottom. Then total darkness came.

As he thinks about those frightening moments, he realizes that he has been saved as by a miracle. One more miracle. This is already the third time that he's escaped from drowning in the nick of time.

Ten-year-olds Vladimir Titov, Viktor Dymov and Tolya Sheludkov, pals in and out of school, often spent an afternoon in search of adventure. One afternoon they wandered along the river, catching trout and following the tracks of wild animals. Tolya suggested they cross the river, for they had just learned to swim. But Vladimir and Viktor were afraid of the wild current. 'OK, I'll do it by myself', Tolya had said, full of bravado, and his friends soon saw him rapidly float downstream. Tolya swam as fast as he could and was already close to the other shore, when he disappeared under water. He had blacked out, and when he regained consciousness he found himself on the river bank.

Two years after that incident Tolya found himself on the river bank again, this time with his father, Leonid. Dad had his usual bottle of vodka handy and he shared it with his son. Leonid had become giddy and proposed they go for a swim, not sensing the danger of the rapid river. At first they both enjoyed it, Tolya jumping on to his Dad's back and both of them slinging mud. But they gradually got away from the river bank, and soon Tolya noticed he couldn't reach bottom anymore. He tried to grab for his Dad, but he too fell over and disappeared under water. Dad was strong and soon reached shore, but Tolya was sucked under by a powerful eddy.

He still remembered the last time he reached the surface. How vividly green the world had been and how blue the sky above. It had been strange and wonderful. He hadn't been afraid of death so close at hand.

But he hadn't died. As he was sucked under again his feet bumped on something heavy, and he felt his strength returning. He managed to grasp a large tree trunk and hold on for dear life, and the trunk soon deposited him on the river bank.

Thinking about those previous scary moments, Tolya knows for sure: it was God who had saved him from drowning . . . three times. Tolya usually is not afraid of anything or anybody, but now he trembles at the thought of his life being in danger all the time. Sure, God has saved him three times, but would He do it a fourth? Unless Tolya changed his life? His father was already dead. For six days he had been unconscious after yet another drinking bout, and all his children had stood around, seeing their father die an alcoholic death. And Tolya's friend Vladimir Titov had died eight years ago in a street fight. Tolya too had lived like an animal. Hell would be awaiting him when he died, he knew it.

His mother was a Christian who often attended the secret worship services of the pentecostal congregation in Arsenyev, the big town close to Chuguyevka, and she had often warned Tolya about his life. When still a child he had accompanied her, but beyond his own brothers and sisters, the services had been attended only by a few old

women. When his mother noticed that as early as the age
of twelve he had begun drinking and keeping bad company,
she persuaded her husband to leave the Soviet Far East
province of Primorski. She hoped that in a Christian
congregation with more young people Tolya and the other
children would fare better. And so the family travelled more
than five thousand miles west, and in 1968 settled at the
Bay of Rostov, east of the Black Sea. It had been a good
decision for Tolya's younger brothers and sisters, who had
all attended the closest pentecostal church in Azov. But 'big'
Tolya had followed his own road, in matters of faith
following his father's example, caring for neither faith nor
church. After seventeen years in the army as a professional
soldier, his father had resigned and also handed in his
communist party card. He'd seen it all: the party was
nothing but corruption and violence. Yet behind his
decision were traces of honourable motives. He had often
said, 'You can't step aside for the rottenness in society.
Sometimes you have to defend the good with force.' Like
his father, Tolya was tough and quick-fisted; he hated
injustice and was quick to defend the cause of the weak.
For instance, once in Azov a group of about twenty-five
students from the agricultural college, looking for trouble,
had spotted Tolya and two of his friends. But Tolya and
his mates had not been afraid, and when the group
continued to bully them, they grabbed some heavy sticks
and beat all of their opponents into the hospital. They even
hit the police who tried to intervene. That had been too
much for the authorities. The youngest of the three was
under-age and escaped punishment, and the other two were
fortunate that their punishment was relatively light. The
capable lawyer Tolya's father had engaged managed to limit
the sentence to one year in a labour camp, tough enough
as that was.

In that camp Tolya learned even more about the seamier

sides of life. It was a brutal camp, one in which you couldn't count on surviving without friends. Tolya had been one of the youngest there, his life often in danger, but he survived and after his year went back home. During that year his parents had returned to the province of Primorski, to Sokolovka, a suburb of Chuguyevka. Actually, Tolya had been glad that he could return to that wild area near the Sea of Japan, for here, in that immense taiga, with its towering trees and sweeping branches, he quickly felt at home again.

Camp life had changed him. He had matured, but had also become embittered. And yet he had not lost his drive to defend the weak. A short time ago Sergeant Kavalchuk of the local secret police had pointed a pistol at him. Without a trace of fear Tolya had walked up to him and kicked the weapon out of the sergeant's hands. The pistol flew far away, and before the sergeant knew what was happening, he found himself on the ground as a result of a brutal blow to his jaw. Tolya knew he had done the right thing.

Tolya isn't afraid, ever, except perhaps for that one time, just about five years ago. The memory of that terrible night now makes him shrivel up with fear again.

In late August 1975 he had married Olga Drozdova, a neighbour, and at first they had lived with Tolya's mother. Once, in the middle of the night, when Tolya lay awake, looking up at the clear star-filled sky, a dark shadow appeared in front of the window. Tolya at first thought it was a cloud, but then he looked more closely. He felt afraid, for this was no cloud but a man! A giant, black figure! Paralysed with fear he waited for something to happen. The man came closer, right through the window and wall. Tolya knew it was a spirit and he wanted to scream but he couldn't produce one sound. The black figure was taller than the window, more than six feet tall, and blacker than any night.

He came very close, and Tolya felt his throat tighten and his chest flatten.

But suddenly a brand-new thought flashed through his head. He saw a cross! Should he make the sign of a cross? But he had never been in an Orthodox church and didn't know how to do it. He tried to lift his hand but he couldn't move it. While this thought of the cross surfaced, something strange happened: the black spirit disappeared instantly and dissolved into the darkness of the night. Now Tolya could move again. He thrashed wildly and wanted to leave the room, afraid of the return of the spirit.

His raw cry cut the still of the night. Olga woke up and saw her husband sit up in bed, his face covered with sweat. He cried out incomprehensibly. Tolya couldn't explain what he had seen. In fits and starts he kept repeating: 'He was here! He came through the window! Mother! We have to see Mother!'

Olga tried to calm him down. 'You had a dream. Your mother is sleeping, it's the middle of the night.' Tolya grew silent; he couldn't explain it to Olga. Nobody would believe him, only his mother Tatyana might understand and help him. She had remained a Christian all these years. She had kept praying for Tolya and the other children. But he let his young wife persuade him and tried to fall asleep again. Of course he didn't sleep a wink. He kept jumping out of bed, fearing that the black spirit was coming back.

At the crack of dawn he and Olga went to his mother, and he told her everything, down to the smallest detail. She listened and shook her head. How her son reminded her of her husband, Leonid, who had been a good person but had thought matters of church and faith in God a lot of nonsense. Tolya was on the same wicked road. She had tears in her eyes at the story of her son, tears of sorrow but also of joy. For her the event was clear: God was calling her child! Softly she said, 'Tolya, my son, God is calling you. The devil became afraid because you are connected to God. That cross you had to think of, that's your salvation!'

Olga was astonished at this story. She didn't understand a word of it. Her parents were atheists and she herself had always been an exemplary member of the communist youth movement.

Afterwards, nobody talked about that frightening experience again. Tolya wanted to forget, but the memory pursued him, willy-nilly. After Juliane was born, he remained sober for a few weeks, but soon he could not resist temptation. The average forest worker would stay in the forest a few days at a time, but in the summer Tolya stayed away for weeks, too drunk to return home.

All those memories flood through Tolya as he lies on that island in the middle of the Ussuri river. His life has meant so little: retreats to the wild; retreats into alcohol; vague ideas about justice and righteousness. He often neglects Olga and little Juliane. And in a few weeks another baby is due.

Slowly he gets up, a little less dizzy already. And then he makes a mighty vow: He, Anatoli Leonidovich Sheludkov, will no longer serve the black satanic powers which have invaded his bedroom and also his heart. God has saved him from drowning three times, and he knows that a fourth time in the water would be fatal. Aloud he says, 'From today, 25th August 1980, I shall not drink one more drop of alcohol. I shall also refrain from smoking and swearing.'

Tolya knows he will stick by his decision. The river will be the border between the past and future. Carefully he picks a safe route to shore and makes his way home to care for his family, to become a real husband and father. But the closer he comes, the more he becomes afraid that Olga might not want him back.

At first Olga doesn't believe his promises. 'I've heard that before', she says contemptuously. But Tolya keeps his word. Svetlana is born on 8th September, and it's not the only day Tolya is at home. He works for weeks to make the necessary repairs to the house, sawing and hammering, always sober now. To Olga's great surprise even his language has improved, although he still has a temper and raises his fists on occasion. But he leaves alcohol alone, and does everything possible to prove that he is truly a changed person.

2
Visitors from Central Asia

In early February of 1981, little Svetlana is already five months old. Since the birth of his daughter Tolya is home more regularly. Even though he and Olga still have their difficulties together, undeniably something good has happened in the life of the forest worker from Sokolovka.

One day Tolya learns that his mother has visitors, a rarity in this area, especially in winter with its sub-zero temperatures. The visitors seem to have come from Central Asia, and Tolya wonders what they want in this isolated corner of the world. After work he first returns home and hugs his two daughters, and after the evening meal makes his way to his parent's home without telling Olga why.

From a distance he can already see the living room lit up. No sooner does he enter the house, than his mother says excitedly, 'We have visitors from the pentecostal church in Akhangaran, near Tashkent.' Tolya keeps his face neutral as he enters the living room to meet two men of about his own age. How different they look from the other men he knows. In Primorski almost everyone looks suspicious and hostile. These two have clear, friendly eyes and open faces. Even before Tolya opens his mouth the two men kiss him. '*Slava Bogu, brat* . . . Praise the Lord, brother, we thank you that we're welcome in this house.' They introduce themselves as Yegor Betcher and Anatolia Khokha, but Tolya hardly hears them, surprised as he is with this brotherly greeting. He isn't a baptist or pentecostal, right? Why do they call him 'brother?' Maybe his mother hasn't told them that he is an unbelieving sinner.

Tolya sits down and notices that those two young Christians accept him as he is. His curiosity grows, even though he tries not to betray it. His face remains sombre and without emotion, as always. Dark and angular Anatoli Khokha is an Armenian, while blond Yegor Betcher has roots in Germany. They're familiar with this region, for they have spent a good deal of their childhood in Warfolomeyevka, about thirty miles west of Chuguyevka. They have also lived as Tolya has, heeding neither the commandments of God nor of men.

But now they are pentecostals, from the Akhangaran church. It is a very special congregation, consisting of young men and women who hold all things in common, together building the houses they live in. Tolya is puzzled when they tell him that they want to live as 'the first Christian church did'.

He marvels at what he hears. Men and women this young? That's quite a difference from the group of the few old women to which his mother belongs, which has nothing to offer him. His amazement grows when he hears of their plans to move the whole congregation to this area. The two of them are searching for a place to live for about a hundred men, women and children. 'What's got into these people?' Tolya asks himself. 'Who would want to live in this place of savages? Primorski began as a place for exiles. It's not an ideal location for Christians now, is it?'

The objections of this powerful forestry worker are met with even greater enthusiasm on the part of Yegor and Anatoli. 'Don't worry, we'll be at home here', they say. 'Moreover, we also have a task. We want to show people here the love of God, through our actions and by telling them about the Gospel of love and redemption.'

After a simple meal Mother Tatyana serves tea, and then Yegor Betcher tells their story. Tolya pays close attention, for it's as if Yegor holds a mirror before him. Yegor also loves nature and the animals from around here. He tells them, 'Central Asia has always remained a hostile country for me, hot and dry and not enough variety. I love the short, almost subtropical summers and the long and severe winters of Siberia.' His talk is gentle and his mouth betrays childlike emotions as he describes nature and recalls his past. Yet his deep blue eyes and white bushy eyebrows indicate the fearlessness of a born adventurer.

'I was born in 1955, in the hamlet of Azad to the north of Kazakhstan. Just before I was born my mother had been converted while visiting relatives in Chelyabinsk, a city near the Ural mountains. She had joined a pentecostal assembly. My father Georg remained a catholic, not an active one mind you, but he had decided never to change religion. His own mother had impressed that decision upon him. Dad kept saying, 'You've got to be content to live a good life to earn a chair near the gates of heaven.' He had been a good man, even though he was an alcoholic.

'Mother was a very lonely Christian. The pentecostal congregation in Chelyabinsk was five hundred miles from Azad, too far for regular attendance. In 1963 the leaders of the congregation were imprisoned, and almost all the other members escaped to the Soviet Far East, as far away as they could. They took the train and literally travelled to the end of the track, Warfolomeyevka in those days, for the line had not yet been extended to Chuguyevka.

'They sent us letters from there, and in 1964 Mother persuaded Dad to move to Primorski too. I was nine then and barely remember the long eleven day journey. The move became a nightmare for me, for I didn't know anybody in that distant place, not even the children of other German families, for I had never accompanied Mother to the assembly in Chelyabinsk.

'Dad found a good job in the aerospace industry and I

began attending school. The other students knew just by looking at my blond hair and blue eyes, that I wasn't Russian. They soon found out that my ancestors had come from Germany, which for them still meant Hitler and Nazis and fascists. Most people in Warfolomeyevka were easily influenced by the communist party. Every time the paper contained an article about fascists, or the theatre showed a war movie, I would pay the price. I lived two miles out of the town, and somewhere a group of boys would be waiting to beat me up. I managed to find another road, much longer but also much more beautiful, right through the taiga. I fell in love with the forests full of wild flowers and fruits. But I also came to hate my peers more all the time. If they couldn't catch me on the road, they'd wait for me at school. They called me fascist even though they didn't even know the meaning of the word, only repeating a word they had heard.

'I hated those stupid bullies. I was small and slender, and all by myself. They were tall, strong and always in a bunch. Often I came home full of bruises and with my clothes torn.

'Eventually the abuse lessened, mainly because of some older boys who began to defend me. I didn't know them, but they proved to be children of other German families who had escaped to this region as well. These Christians were very afraid of the KGB, and they had decided not to take their children to the secret worship services. In truth, each family lived much on its own so that they would not draw attention to their being Christians and Germans. That's why I never got to know the boys from those other German families.

'You get used to everything in the end, even verbal abuse, beatings and ongoing discrimination. I discovered that family rules for decency were invitations for immediate abuse here. Survival in this uncivilized part of Siberia meant putting up your fists. I still remember when my attitude changed, one day when I was twelve years old. A gang of Russian school boys yanked the scarves off the heads of some German girls while abusing them with the foulest of language. My anger made me forget my fear. Furious, I ran into the group and kicked and hit where I could. Of course I got as much as I dished out, but from that moment on I had no fear. I knew that only my fists could get me respect.

'From that day I lived by the rules of the jungle, spreading fear and even gaining a few friends. I began a life of street fights, drunkenness and other behaviour I thought necessary to maintain my reputation as a tough teenager. I wasn't the only one – other German immigrant kids lived the same way.

'When in 1968 the leaders of the pentecostal congregation were freed after five years of imprisonment, they didn't recognize their own children any more. Quickly they decided to return to "civilization", which for most meant moving back to Central Asia.

'Our family stayed on in Primorski for another three years. We weren't that much a part of the congregation, for my mother was the only Christian in the family. However, my father and mother followed the example of the others in 1971. My dad found a house and a job close to Frunze, the capital of Kirghisi.

'I was sixteen and applied at the technical school, where I got to know four other boys like me. Alcohol, sex and violence were our delights. I lived with those four in the city and rarely came home any more. Yet my mother continued to pray for me.'

Tolya gives Yegor his full attention. How similar to his own story: Yegor's mother also the only believer in the family, his father an alcoholic and Yegor himself a wild animal.

When Yegor takes a break he gently observes, 'I could tell you more, but are you interested?'

Tolya nods and Anatoli Khokha says, 'Yegor, I think you should tell him how you became a Christian.' Yegor smiles and strokes his chin, doubting that Tolya will believe him, so unbelievable is the story. But then he thinks to himself, 'Maybe God will use my story.'

'At four o'clock on the morning of 15th January 1974, still asleep, I became aware of someone lightly tapping my shoulder. Slowly I woke up. Maybe I had slept in, for the room was lit up? But after I rubbed my eyes I saw a tall white figure next to my bed. I pulled the blanket over me, trembling all over and cold with fear. At first I thought I was dreaming, but when I bit my finger I knew that what was happening was as real as the pain in it. Carefully I lifted the edge of the sheet. The "White Man" still stood there. His head almost reached the ceiling and he looked at me without speaking a word. I threw myself around, pulled up my knees and pushed my face into the pillow, holding the blankets tight around me. But the White Man easily pulled them off me and grasped my one shoulder. His strength was great, yet his touch was gentle. I felt the enormous power that turned me around, as a mother turns her child. There, I lay on my back and looked straight into the eyes of that strange, white figure.

'Slowly my eyes got used to the bright light. The man didn't seem as fearsome as I had first thought. His face was friendly and his voice, soft and deep, said, "Follow me", and it was neither a question nor a compelling commandment. He stuck out his hand, and a larger one I had never seen before. Suddenly I felt a great desire to hold that large hand, but I could only grasp two fingers of it. While I held them, carefully and shyly, I felt all my fears draining away. A warm glow filled my body. The tall man turned around but he held his hand behind him. Like a small child I followed him, still clutching those two fingers. He wore a long white robe and I had to be careful not to step on it. Together we approached the door, but in spite of the fact that he was much taller than the top of it he made no motion to bend down. He went straight through it, and through the wall above it. I followed him to the threshold, where suddenly he disappeared and darkness reappeared. Slowly my eyes got used to the dark again, and I could see the outlines of the furniture and the door.

'Then I saw that I was not alone. Against the doorpost leaned a revolting figure, black and reaching only to my chest. The moment I saw him he took both my hands in an iron grip with his sweaty, black hands. Full of despair I looked for the White Man, but he was not to be seen any more. The little monster had an evil face which changed constantly, one moment appearing friendly, his mouth a broad grin, the next furious and showing his huge eye-teeth. His icecold, blue-grey eyes had a penetrating look. The peaceful atmosphere of just a moment ago had disappeared totally. With a steely voice the dwarf asked, "Yegor, you have served me for nineteen years. Why did you follow that man today?" I didn't answer him and tried to struggle out of the grip of that monster. I put my foot against the door post and pulled as hard as I could. Finally he let go and disappeared into the dark, after a last angry glance in my direction.

'Trembling with fear I went back to bed and hid under the blankets. Afraid and confused I awaited the dawn. Only then did my fear begin to subside a bit. I quickly dressed and escaped to the outside, to my job. I would have liked to go back to my mother but she lived twenty miles away. But that evening, as soon as I could get away, I visited my family. Mother looked startled as soon as she saw me, and immediately knew that something had happened. As I told my story she had tears in her eyes and shook her head. She put her hands on mine and said, "Yegor, it is God who is calling you. You must follow Him!" Those were the only words she could say.

'For the first time ever I prayed aloud beside my mother. Both of us thanked God for the love which is always stronger than the worst evil in the world.

'The next day I went back to my friends to tell them the wonderful story of that night. They listened, it is true, but when I told them I had become a Christian, they laughed at me. Shortly after I packed my bags and rented a room not far from my job.

'The news of my conversion travelled fast. I told everyone who wanted to hear. With one exception, my brothers and sisters soon followed my example, but my father only shook his head. He believed my story but kept saying that it wasn't right for a person to change religion just like that.

'My life turned around completely after that. I got to know many more young believers and discovered that the Christian life is not boring at all. After my meeting with the "White Man" I also lost my fear of the authorities, even though they tried to change my mind. My father was called to the police station. The district police chief asked him if his son had lost his marbles. "He's acting strangely and he is confusing a lot of people." Father felt ashamed on account of me. When he came home he angrily called me many names and spat out, "It's because of you that I have to go to the police. Is that what conversion means? If you keep on living like that, I don't need you as a son any more!"

'It wasn't too long before my unconverted friends went from bad to worse. They began to steal and commit fraud and all four of them landed in gaol. One day my father said to the chief, "My boy is home with me, and his friends are in gaol. Even the children of the party chairman are in trouble. Maybe my son isn't as crazy as you think." Shortly after that he said to me, "Son, it's good you have changed. Keep it up.'"

Tolya, his mother and Anatoli listen to Yegor Betcher's story with their eyes glued to his face. The giant from Sokolovka has tears in his eyes at the end. How similar to Yegor's his own life has been! He ponders the words of the miraculous "White Man". He repeats them over and over in his head, "Follow me".

Tolya knows that it is already very late, but he cannot leave without responding to these words. Indeed, he too wants to grasp that hand and follow Jesus.

Neither Yegor nor Anatoli has to urge him any further. He falls to his knees. With tears, and interrupted by long pauses, he pours out his heart, cataloguing all his failures, his anger, his sins. Only then does his heart grow quiet. Very softly and awkwardly he asks, 'Jesus, may I follow You?'

3
Soldier in the Soviet Army

Frunze, 1975

A year after his conversion Yegor Betcher was drafted into
military service. His life had changed a lot. Earlier the idea
of conscientious objection would never have entered his
mind, not even when remembering that as part of the
German ethnic group in the Soviet Union he could look
forward to a hard life in the army. But now he would have
to think the issue through, for the most important issue in
his life was obedience to God's laws.

The small and informal pentecostal assembly to which
Yegor now belonged faithfully pointed every boy of draft
age to the sixth commandment, 'Thou shalt not kill'.
Killing in wartime or out of self-defence might perhaps be
less sinful than murder, but killing is killing, and God
emphatically forbids it. Moreover, each soldier had to swear
obedience to the military command, and with a hand
touching the red flag solemnly promise to defend the
fatherland to the bitter end. Members of a Free Evangelical
Church (the Soviet name for pentecostal assemblies) cannot
accept having to swear any oath, but to pledge allegiance
to an atheist regime was even more unthinkable.

Yegor found the choice easy. He knew what his refusal
could mean, but his faith had continued to grow stronger
since his meeting with the 'White Man'. He had discovered already that he could count on complete protection
when walking in Jesus's footsteps and obeying Him in
all things.

Twenty-year-old Yegor made his objections public the

very day he had to report for duty, but the duty officer pretended not to hear him and assigned the blond German to an armoured division. Oath-taking took place a few days later. All recruits meekly obeyed, except Yegor. 'The first day I already said that I would not bear arms and would not swear the oath. I am a Christian and I obey the Scriptures.' His voice was soft, but the words were convincing enough to cause all heads to turn in his direction, the other boys with fear and the duty officer white with anger. The latter soon recovered and threatened to lock him up, but Yegor refused to change his mind. He was taken to the camp commandment, clearly a KGB man, who said, 'We won't bother with you here. We have a special unit for you. For the time being you're assigned to a labour battalion.'

Soon Yegor found himself transported to an army base close to the Caspian Sea. There he joined others who would or could not do normal military duty: fundamentalist Muslims, convicted criminals, malingerers and a few believers like himself.

Every day Yegor had to report to KGB officers. The KGB is the largest secret service in the world, and it has a special section that guards the political and ideological reliability of the military. The officers first tried conversation to get Yegor to change his mind, but he wasn't afraid, and continued to talk freely about God and the Scriptures. Soon the conversations became torrents of abuse. Next, when it became clear that words would not persuade this young Christian from Frunze, they tried physical violence. Ordinary soldiers were egged on to beat and kick Yegor whenever they felt like it. The assaults steadily grew longer and more frequent. The night before his group was to swear the oath, they tortured him until 3 am. They twisted his arms behind his back and pushed his face into the ground. But Yegor was not afraid of them, and he was not prepared to sell out his principles, not even in the face of all the pain.

The next morning he didn't appear on parade, and that afternoon he was transferred to another nearby base, where they told him that he could expect a gaol term.

At least they now left him in peace. The army authorities had finally concluded that he would not change. Until his court martial they made him work right beside the other soldiers, who had developed a deep respect for his perseverance, and he established good relations with most of them.

One day they had to unload a freight train. A crane lifted timber from it to be stacked next to the tracks. Yegor and three other soldiers stood on the wagon to attach the chains. Gradually the tempo increased. The boys worked hard and they soon knew exactly what to do.

But then a terrible accident happened. One of the soldiers had probably become a bit careless, for just when the load of several thousand kilos swerved right above Yegor's head, a chain gave way. With a loud rumble the heavy timber fell down. The other soldiers managed to jump aside, but Yegor jumped too late. One plank bumped his chest and threw him backwards off the wagon. His right shoulder hit a railroad tie and he remained motionless. His mates quickly ran to help him, knowing that he had been badly hurt. His shoulder blade stood at an angle to his body and his arm was completely bent out of shape. Quickly they put him on a stretcher and a jeep took him to the small base hospital. Immediately he was put into the emergency room. After a nurse had cut away his shirt, the real damage became obvious. No fewer than eleven doctors, nurses and officers crowded around him. At first the pain almost made Yegor unconscious, but as soon as someone touched his shoulder the pain surged up. Sometimes he drifted into unconsciousness, and yet he clearly heard what the officers were discussing. They wanted to have him transported to a larger hospital for an operation.

Yegor kept praying and felt the close presence of God through it all. Suddenly a warm glow streamed through his body. He was reminded of the experience of a year ago, when he grasped the hand of the 'White Man'. But now the force of it was even stronger. All his limbs tingled, but his shoulder even more. Yegor noticed that something miraculous was happening. He felt his shoulder crack inside, but he noticed no pain. It took only a few seconds and before anyone could stop him, Yegor slid off the treatment table.

The eleven men couldn't believe their eyes. They first stared at his shoulder, and then approached to feel it carefully. Then they grasped it firmly. No twisted bones could be seen! Yegor, the doctors, the nurses, the officers, they all saw it with their own eyes: the shoulder was normal and healed. Everything was firm and back in its proper place, without even a scar! Everyone was speechless.

Soldier Yegor received a new shirt and was returned to his barracks, where his comrades sat sadly together, still depressed by the accident. But when the 'patient' entered, laughing and completely healed, they too could not believe their eyes. Yegor looked as rosy and healthy as before the accident, and they all wanted to know how that was possible. They crowded around him. Yegor told them what had happened, in simple words. 'God has performed a miracle. He healed me. The officers around me saw with their own eyes how the broken bones found their proper place again. God is alive. He is my Lord!'

They all wanted to inspect his shoulder, having seen what a mess it had been. And now, not even a scar! The dormitory fell silent. Now no one ridiculed Yegor's faith any more. From that day on they listened attentively when he spoke about the Scriptures. No one doubted his miraculous healing. The only thing that stopped many from choosing to serve God was the risk of a confrontation with the KGB.

The day after the accident Yegor was told to report to the chief physician of the hospital. The man was alone, and he carefully closed his office door behind Yegor. Yegor knew that he had been greatly upset in the treatment room yesterday.

He asked the soldier to stretch out on the table, and he carefully examined his shoulder again. A long silence followed. Even after he motioned Yegor to get dressed, he stared silently at the grey clouds over the fading yellow curtains which shielded the examination room from curious onlookers.

Timidly Yegor waited for the military doctor to tell him what to do next. When the man turned to him, he looked the soldier straight in the eye and asked him, 'Soldier Betcher, can you tell me exactly what happened yesterday?' Yegor smiled uncomfortably and replied, 'Comrade Major, you were there. I don't know any more than you do. Except, perhaps, one thing: I know for certain that God has healed me.'

The man nodded at the answer he had expected. He walked to the corner of the room. To Yegor's amazement he picked up a guitar and handed it to him. 'Here,' he said, 'I know that you can play this thing. Please sing me a song about God.' Yegor took the instrument and played his favourite, 'Who is our God and Creator?' The doctor listened attentively, and for a moment Yegor thought he saw something glistening in the doctor's eyes, but the man kept his head turned away until the song was finished. And that was the end of the examination. Yegor and that military doctor never met again.

It didn't take long for the news of the miraculous healing to spread throughout the barracks and even through the surrounding villages. One day a lieutenant addressed the soldiers. 'What soldier Betcher has been telling you is not true. He says that God performed a miracle, but that's just a story. I was present and saw with my own eyes how the doctor skilfully treated the wounds of soldier Betcher.' The boys who had been present at the accident and who had seen Yegor's shoulder before and after the healing, knew better. Sadly, this lieutenant had indeed been one of the officers in the emergency room. He had seen how God performed a miracle, but the fear of losing his position made him choose a lie.

Some time later another officer approached Yegor. The event had so touched him that he wanted to hear more about the Bible. 'It is not right to deliberately banish from daily life a God who can perform such a thing', he reasoned. Following a number of talks, officers Leonid Banchikov and Yegor together found a quiet little place in the barracks where they prayed together. Leonid confessed his sins and decided to serve God from then on. But it's not easy for army officers to abandon party and ideology. Banchikov faced a very difficult time after news of his conversion became public.

After more than a year Yegor was given permission to return home on leave. The army authorities couldn't refuse to let him go, for one of the children of his oldest sister, Elvira, had died. Yet the leave was not only a sad event. In fact, those few days at home were to prove crucial for Yegor's future, for at the funeral he met two youth leaders from Central Asian pentecostal congregations, Nikolai Vins from Leninabad and Viktor Walter from Akhangaran. Yegor had heard Viktor's name before, for he too had lived in Primorski for a number of years, and no more than two miles away. He had been five years old then and had lived like Tolya Sheludkov and the other citizens of Primorski: unmannered, uncontrolled and without purpose.

They talked deep into the night. Viktor Walter told his own story about what had happened in his life after he moved to Central Asia with his parents.

A few months after the move he had come to the Lord, together with his brother Vladimir. Soon after he had to join the army, he also refused to bear arms and swear the military oath. They locked him up in psychiatric institutions, and the KGB interrogated him numerous times and accused him of desertion.

Much of Viktor's story paralleled Yegor's. Viktor was also sent to a labour battalion. He too, like Yegor, was seriously injured through an accident. But Viktor stayed in a sick bed for many years, a time he used to read and think about the Bible. The book of Acts made a special impression on him, with its story of the life of the early Christians. They had been opposed constantly, but they had not let the authorities stop them. 'What a difference between their lives and the lives of Christians in the Soviet Union', he had begun to think. 'Why are we Christians here so afraid of the authorities?' He thought a lot about that and the conclusion grew in his heart: 'It has to be possible for Christians in the Soviet Union to live according to the norms of the Bible!'

Viktor came to meet other young Christians who had similar thoughts about the future of the Church. Together they discussed how they could choose other, more biblical roads for themselves. 'We Christians are too weak if we stay separated from each other. That's what our parents demonstrated. They should have taken us to church more. Fortunately God heard their prayers and we are believers now, but we want to prevent our children from having to live through similar dark times. We Christians need each other. Moreover, we are needed as witnesses of Jesus Christ to the atheists and Muslims. Couldn't we be witnesses together? Not only in church but also in daily life? We could be so much more productive for the Kingdom of God if all of us could use our talents to the full.'

Yegor admired the plans of the young Christians from Akhangaran to begin a communal life, but the thought of being part of it himself did not enter his head then.

After a few days he returned to the base. The soldiers counted on him now and Yegor was creative in finding quiet corners to talk with them about the Bible, and to pray with them. Memories of his conversations with Viktor Walter and Nikolai Vins soon faded. Then he got a letter from his mother: she planned to move to Akhangaran. His brother-in-law Anatoli Khokha and his family were also moving, to a village just east of Tashkent. Yegor rejoiced for his mother, for she would have more support from other Christians there. Actually, he himself had looked forward to returning to Frunze after his military service, for he had many friends there who had not come to the faith yet. But now his parental home would be in Akhangaran.

Yegor's military service was coming to a close. Leonid Banchikov, the converted officer, dreaded the moment, for he had been told that heavy times were sure to come after the departure of his brother and friend, Yegor. 'What do you think, Yegor. Can a Christian remain an officer in the army?' Yegor knew what was required of officers: ideological and political purity, and readiness to execute even unreasonable and godless orders. That's why the boy replied, 'No, I don't believe so. You will have to make a choice, Leonid, follow Jesus or remain a professional officer.'

But resigning on the grounds of religious convictions carried with it a gaol term of seven years, and a lot of subsequent career problems.

As it happened, Leonid didn't even get an opportunity to make the choice. Immediately after Yegor's departure he was locked up for weeks and subjected to endless interrogations. He managed to write Yegor two letters, but that was all. Maybe he had abandoned his faith. However, Yegor suspected that the KGB had confiscated additional letters, a common practice meant to isolate Christians from their brothers and sisters.

On his arrival in Akhangaran in 1977, Yegor moved in with his parents. His mother's life had blossomed in the midst of all those young Christians. His father still stubbornly maintained that one ought not to change religions, yet to Yegor's amazement he attended all the services, and he even prayed aloud on occasion. But he could not leave alcohol alone completely, and a year after their arrival he died.

The Akhangaran Christian lifestyle deeply impressed Yegor. Gone were the traditional secretive ways. Worship services were now open to everyone and all things were done together. Christians worked together for one employer. They worked together to build houses. They evangelized together in neighbouring villages and settlements, with the help of shared, ageing motorcycles and cars. They even practised diaconate for old and sick folk, a practice strictly forbidden for the Church in those days.

It truly was a unique experiment! God had begun new labours. The Holy Spirit was finding new ears, speaking through the Word, through dreams and visions. Joel's prophesies were being fulfilled.

Yegor attached himself to the crew that worked in the railway yards. He enjoyed the friendship and unity of the Christian community members in Akhangaran. From now on the Congregation of Jesus Church would no longer play hide and seek, but become the salt and light of the world!

4
Flight to the Far East

Chelyabinsk, 1950

In the 1950s, some Ukrainian evangelists travelled east. Of course they couldn't proselytize openly in those days, but during the time Nikita Khrushchev was in control, and a measure of freedom was in the air, the more active Christians looked for opportunities to evangelize. Most Christians, however, were still paralysed by fear after Stalin's reign of terror, and avoided everything that might renew persecution.

The travelling preachers worked very carefully, taking no unnecessary risks and avoiding visits to homes they knew nothing about. Instead, they would try to discover the name of an old Orthodox believer in an out-of-the-way hamlet, for instance, and drop in for some casual chat. If the host or hostess proved receptive to Bible teaching, family and friends would be invited too. In this way they established a meeting place for Christians and a basis for further evangelism.

That's how Chelyabinsk, a city some nine hundred miles east of Moscow, came to be visited by evangelists. There they encountered a number of German families who had been branded Nazis after World War II and banished to East Siberia. Most of them had been transported out of White Russia and the Ukraine, where they had been granted some measure of religious freedom under the nazi occupation. However, they had stayed away from nazi involvement and were known to be diligent workers. Yet Stalin treated them as traitors. They were held accountable for all of Hitler's crimes, although none of them had even set foot in Germany. Long ago, Catherine the Great had invited their great-great-grandfathers to Russia as guest workers and since then Russia had become their fatherland.

The Ukrainian evangelists belonged to the pentecostal movement which was established in the 1920s through the work of Ivan Voronayev, a Russian who had lived in America. In the first few years after the Revolution the movement grew rapidly, but during the evil Stalin years the work had virtually halted. Hence, these isolated Chelyabinsk Christians heard for the first time that God wanted to pour out the Holy Spirit over His children once more. Following the example of the apostle Paul, these evangelists asked them, 'Did you receive the Holy Spirit when you came to the faith?' Most of them had to say no. While Bible verses pointed to the Holy Spirit providing power, boldness and love, they had no personal experience of them. For instance, they lacked all boldness, paralysed as they were with fear of atheists. Suspicion took the place of love. Each Christian lived for himself, and many were in urgent need of communion with fellow believers.

Actually, they all longed for the Holy Spirit to rule their lives. After only a few days some of them were baptized in the Holy Spirit, and others soon followed. The new group in Chelyabinsk also began to resist the unbiblical demands of the authorities.

These new experiences could not be kept a secret, of course. Colleagues at work, family members and neighbours soon noticed the changes. The resulting renewal of existing Christians managed to attract others who belonged to no church. Soon this new congregation of pentecostals expanded to over five hundred members.

But just about that time Khrushchev began his anti-religion campaign, with the promise that within a few years the last Soviet Union Christian would be an exhibit on TV.

Once more, churches were closed and hundreds of Christians arrested and convicted. In 1962 four pastors of this new congregation were sentenced to five years of hard labour.

The persecution was so severe that none of the other leaders (called deacons) dared to stay around. Without even informing the members of the congregation, they fled to unknown destinations in the middle of the night. The remnant felt abandoned and looked for its leaders, but no one knew their whereabouts. A few believers remained in Chelyabinsk, but most of them took flight as well. The congregation was disbanded for the moment. Some families went south, but others went east as far as they could, to Primorski.

Warfolomeyevka – 1963

Samuel and Frida Walter and their eight children were among the fugitives. For ten days they travelled through inhospitable regions. Vladimir, the eldest son, turned fifteen during the trip, and he still remembers the tension. They had abruptly left in the middle of one spring night, with no more than three suitcases for the whole family. The parents had no idea where they would end up, but in their minds no place could be worse than Chelyabinsk. The train took them through endless snow-covered Siberian plains, through the craggy mountain terrain north of Mongolia, and reached Khabarovsk, the city on the lengthy river Amur which forms the border with China and empties into the Sea of Okhotsk. But they didn't want to stay there either, and so they travelled on south towards Vladivostok, the harbour city on the Sea of Japan. Gradually the country became gentler and the temperature more moderate.

They were within a few hours of arriving in Vladivostok

when Samuel decided to leave this train for another that
would bring them deeper into the province of Primorski.
They stayed on the new train until they reached the final
stop: Warfomoleyevka. There they stood, ten people and
three small suitcases. Fortunately it was spring and the
weather was warm enough. They walked through the
village in the direction of the forest. The little ones were
very tired, and Father and the bigger boys had to carry
them. A short distance after they had left the last houses
behind them they found an abandoned hut where they
unpacked their suitcases.

That same day Father left to look for work and a home.
He stayed away two nights and two days. Vladimir still
remembers how his mother became increasingly worried,
constantly looking out of the window. She would burst out
crying with every thought that he might not return.

Finally she saw him coming. Even from a distance he
called out that he had found shelter and work, a great relief
for all of them after those frightening days in a strange
forest. Samuel Walter had found temporary work with a
blacksmith, and the family had been assigned two rooms
in a tenement building.

Nobody there knew that they were Christians, and they
agreed to keep that information to themselves for a while.
The people around them were brutish and had been taught
to hate the Church with passion. Of course they were totally
ignorant about religion, for nowhere in Primorski was a
church or a Christian to be found.

Some time later the family received word about the other
refugees from Chelyabinsk. The family of one of the four
pastors, Wilhem Friesen, now lived about twenty miles
away, and a few other families had settled together in
Warfolomeyevka. Other families had travelled east for
another hundred and twenty miles.

At the end of the summer Samuel Walter found a job

as crane operator on the railway with his oldest son Vladimir as his helper. Vladimir toiled beneath heavy bags of cement for most of the day, and also learned to be a crane operator himself.

Samuel tried to strengthen contacts with other Christians by occasionally organizing a service. They all agreed to keep their worship a secret. Even their own children would not know, for if they were to share the secret with their school mates, new persecutions would be sure to start here. School only offered them atheistic propaganda. Moreover, school also portrayed Germans as eternal enemies, and children with German parents often had to defend themselves.

The consequence was that their children became more and more estranged from the faith. The children logically concluded that faith wasn't relevant outside the home, and quickly adopted the lifestyle examples the Russians provided. Soon they hit back when they were hit, and developed into a gang of street fighters, partly for self-defence, and partly to gain peer respect. They also seemed to delight in adopting the very lifestyle their parents warned them about: dancing, the cinema, girls and especially excessive drinking.

In 1967, after five years of labour camp, Wilhelm Friesen was released. He travelled to the province of Primorski for a joyous reunion with his wife and children. Samuel and Frida Walter came out to welcome their old friend and pastor. Of course they travelled the twenty miles without their children, for congregational contacts were strictly for adults.

Wilhelm Friesen was dismayed by this fearful attitude. It didn't take him long to notice how his own daughter, Anna, who had confessed Christ before his arrest, lived as if God did not exist. She went dancing, regularly attended the cinema, and lived like all the other girls in the village. Samuel told him that all the children of the Christians had become apostate, including his own two sons Vladimir and Viktor.

Wilhelm had experienced the near presence of God so much in the labour camp that he couldn't understand why the others had let things go this far. He suggested, 'Let's all move closer together and start a congregation, or perhaps we should move to a different town where our children can begin a new life and we can involve them in congregational affairs.'

Friesen remained in Primorski for only a few weeks, then quickly departed for Central Asia. The members of the congregation who had fled there were in much better shape, for they had not lost their children.

Akhangaran – 1967

Within a year all German families had moved from Primorski to Central Asia, except for the Betcher family, for Georg Betcher was not a Christian and didn't see the need to move. To their father's sorrow, at first Vladimir and Viktor Walter also objected to the move. After all, they had their friends here and felt at home in the company of fighters, drinkers and party animals. But they made so much trouble that the police chief called in their father. 'Mister Walter, if you don't take those boys with you, I'll put them in gaol.' For Samuel this threat was a godsend, for now he had a good reason to force his sons to come along.

In fact, the boys, aged seventeen and nineteen, were the first to leave for Akhangaran, in December 1967. Shortly thereafter the rest of the family followed. Wilhelm Friesen had become pastor of a small pentecostal church, and here everyone attended. Viktor and Vladimir came too. Actually, they liked meeting others their own age. Slowly it dawned on them that religion wasn't just a hobby for old people.

Increasingly they grew ashamed of all the things they had done and the pain they had caused their parents. After a few months Vladimir went forward in a worship service and confessed all his sins to two elders. This great big boy cried like a baby. He now realized that forgiveness of sins through the completed work of Jesus Christ was the only road to salvation. Within a week his brother Viktor followed his example.

A few days after Viktor's conversion one of the families organized a youth evening, a celebration for all those present. Following the example of their elders, the youth all knelt down during the communal prayer (where all voices pray at the same time, according to Russian pentecostal tradition). During this cacophony of voices Vladimir felt enormous gratitude and love overflow his heart. With tears streaming down his face he began to praise and thank God. 'You have been baptized in the Holy Spirit', the others told him. Vladimir didn't quite understand the remark, so Wilhelm Friesen explained to him that the Holy Spirit was finding a way to guide the whole of Vladimir's life. With the pastor the boy knelt down once again and invited the Holy Spirit into his life. A glow of power and love now took total possession of him, and he didn't even notice that the words of his prayer were in another language that he couldn't even understand.

'We welcome you most warmly', Wilhelm Friesen said. 'We can't explain what happens when the Holy Spirit fills your life, but when it happens to you it's a wonderful secret.'

That first period of time in Akhangaran was one of rich blessings. Compared to other parts of the Soviet Union there was a lot of freedom here, and believers came to Akhangaran from the far corners of the district. The congregation grew and so did contact with other pentecostal churches.

But then, the documents of that earlier court case five years ago in Chelyabinsk arrived. The local KGB immediately launched an investigation and discovered that the sister congregations of Akhangaran, Angren and Tashkent were growing 'disturbingly' fast. The growing pentecostal youth movement bothered them especially. They looked for a provocation to derail the influence of the leaders. Leonid Brezhnev had come to power in the meantime and he had given the KGB complete authority to force all believers, Muslims and Christians, to register with the government. However, fearing the large number of Muslims in Central Asia, the judges here used the tried and true method of attacking the Germans as Nazis, reviving the pattern of the 1950s.

The so-called nazi case came to trial in Angren. Pentecostal leaders were supposed to have had close contact with Hitler's SS and fought side by side with the German army. After assembling all 'conclusive documents' eight pastors were arrested, among them ex-prisoner and Akhangaran pastor Wilhelm Friesen.

The showcase trial got underway in April 1969, and was featured on the front pages of all East Asia newspapers. Angren's walls hung full of posters with the names of the eight 'fascists' and their 'crimes'. One of them wasn't even German, and had lost a leg fighting as a Russian soldier against the nazi army. But Alexander Bykov had been a member of a predominantly German pentecostal assembly and that was good enough. The public was so aroused that the accused had to be protected. Crowds stood at the court building yelling, 'Down with fascists, down with Nazis. Hang them all.' The public galleries inside the court house were crowded with people who had been riled up especially for the occasion.

Viktor Walter sat in the court house too, in the company of the other family members of the accused. He witnessed how his gentle and wise pastor was brutally chased through the court room. He noticed how another leader, too weak to walk, received heavy kicks against his legs. Fathers of large families were beaten in their faces when they denied having committed the crimes they were accused of.

Wilhelm Friesen was ill enough to warrant a doctor giving him periodic injections to revive him a bit, so that he could answer the questions put to him. Viktor Walter, that former street fighter turned Christian less than a year ago, was enraged at having to witness all this in silence. But the brothers in the dock helped change his feelings of revenge into pity for the accusers. Politely and with great dignity they responded to the vilest accusations. Their only defence was the love of Christ. They didn't even try to justify themselves when each of them was given opportunity for a last word. One after the other simply stated that they felt it an honour to be able to suffer for the Name of Jesus Christ.

'That's how I want to be', Viktor Walter thought. 'These men are not afraid of the consequences of obeying God. They are prepared to relinquish everything for the sake of the Gospel, even wives and children. They know that God is on their side and that He will defend their cause, even if it means five years of prison or more.'

Right in the midst of that hostile crowd Viktor bowed his head and softly prayed, 'Lord God, I want to dedicate my whole life to You. I don't want to keep anything back. If it is Your will, let me walk this road too. Your will be done! Your Kingdom come! Amen.'

5
Conscientious Objector
Viktor Walter

Semipalatinsk, 1969

Shortly after this so-called anti-nazi trial the KGB visited Viktor Walter. They asked him what his plans were regarding army service. He had already received his physical examination and could expect his orders at any time. Viktor answered that he had to think about it a bit more and that he would give them his answer as soon as possible. He went to the remaining church elders for counsel, but they had become so afraid that they were reluctant to make suggestions that could endanger themselves or others. Viktor had to make this tough decision entirely on his own. He reminded himself of the attitudes of the eight condemned men who did not want to hold back anything in obeying God's Word, and then he knew what to do. He wrote the following letter to the army authorities.

Dear commandant,
I have been called up for military service, but I am not prepared to bear arms or swear the military oath. I am a Christian and the Bible forbids me to kill and swear. Moreover, I simply cannot defend the cause of communism with my last drop of blood.
Respectfully, Viktor Samuelovich Walter.

In a few days he received a call to report to the Tashkent staff officers. The reception there was anything but friendly, and no one even tried to change his mind. His letter had been clear and only one reply was possible: a sentence for desertion.

During the transportation to Semipalatinsk, a secret base for nuclear testing located about nine hundred miles north of Akhangaran, he had some time to think about his decision. Once there, he composed a second statement of his refusal to bear arms or swear an oath. The local military authorities, being convinced that he would not change his mind, sent him to a psychiatric institution close to the base. But after a day of exhausting discussions he was moved again. Viktor didn't know where he was headed, whether to a labour camp or a special army base. He was under heavy guard for the few days of the trip, and no one told him anything. He finally arrived in the psychiatric hospital of Alma-Ata, about eight hundred miles south of Semipalatinsk.

This sane, healthy nineteen-year-old was locked up with seriously ill psychiatric patients. Many of those drooling and incontinent people acted like caged animals, roaring wildly and sometimes physically attacking others. Viktor only had a few conversations with a psychiatrist, who was so under the influence of the KGB that he said, 'As long as you believe in God, you are still unbalanced. Only if you renounce God will I declare you cured.'

After a period of this horror, Viktor was taken back to Semipalatinsk, under heavy guard. Again they asked him to swear the military oath. He refused without a moment's thought. The KGB brought him back every day, each day with the same question, and each day Viktor's answer was the same. After one full month the officers said, 'Okay, you don't want to listen. Back to the psychiatrist once more, before we sentence you.'

Again Viktor was taken away under heavy guard, this time to Tashkent, not far from Akhangaran where he lived, to a military hospital with a psychiatric wing. Even though the patients here were in better shape, the building looked more like a gaol than a hospital. He was also not allowed to receive visitors.

Viktor was incarcerated with young boys who had been treated so badly during the first few weeks of military service that their minds had become unhinged. He shared a dormitory with mentally ill officers and malingerers. He heard tales of sadistic officers who wouldn't hesitate to murder soldiers. A fellow prisoner told Viktor, 'I prefer a labour camp to the army. At least there you understand the prison rules, but the army is total chaos and the officers exploit the situation.' Viktor had occasion to remember those words later.

After many conversations with psychiatrists who were also KGB officers Viktor learned that he would be court martialled. The report about him said that he wasn't ill and didn't suffer from psychiatric abnormalities. Viktor agreed, of course, but he didn't agree with the next section of the report. 'Soldier Walter is not a believer. He's only a malingerer who refused to do his military duty. He must be judged according to article 249a of the penal code.' Viktor knew what that meant: three to seven years of labour camp. Pending his court martial, Viktor was assigned to a labour battalion in Semipalatinsk, where he was to help with the construction of officers' quarters.

One thing life in the psychiatric hospitals had taught VIktor was the need for even greater constancy in prayer. He felt himself safely in God's hands, and discovered that God regularly provided him with friends, including some in Semipalatinsk, young men with whom he could openly talk about his faith. He discovered a great hunger for talk about God and faith. However, the officers tried to get a smear campaign going against him, telling everyone that he was a fascist and a dangerous enemy of the state. The fact that Viktor openly witnessed to his faith made the KGB even angrier, and Viktor sensed that he would get the maximum punishment of seven years.

He worked as mason in the labour battalion, in the depth of winter when it was far too cold for such work. One morning sleet pelted down from the skies, and even those cruel guards thought it was too dangerous for the boys to stay up on the scaffolding. The soldiers were allowed to go inside to wait for an improvement in the weather. One of the supervisors told Viktor that he first had to clean up some materials and then could come down too. Viktor continued his work, on the fifth floor high above other buildings. He had a fine view of the surroundings. The work wasn't difficult as long as he was careful. His thoughts were back home. Viktor worried about the Akhangaran congregation, for after the show trial older Christians had become afraid once more and hardly dared worship together. Would the young people let themselves be intimidated again, in spite of the blessings they had experienced? How much he would have liked to be with them. Then he shifted his attention to meditating about God.

The temperature turned colder and the support for his feet became more slippery. Viktor took great care, but the cold had left his hands and feet without feelings. He carefully carried some empty cement bags and loose timber to the open staircase, but at the edge of it he slipped and fell against the board which served as a fence. It came loose and Viktor dropped down into the hole. It all happened so fast that he couldn't hold on to anything. He fell right past the cement edges of the staircase. Yet he felt as in a dream, without panic or fear, as if floating. Then his body hit the ground with a dull thud and he was unconscious.

When he awoke he found himself in an ambulance. He still didn't understand what had happened and thought he was dreaming. The doctors in the hospital diagnosed a broken back. Fortunately he wasn't paralysed, but he wouldn't be allowed to move for a while, and they fitted him out with a special girdle.

The accident had little influence on the KGB attitude. Viktor asked if they could notify his parents but they curtly refused. The doctors were under instruction to treat him as a criminal waiting to be sentenced.

But God had His own ways to inform his parents. The afternoon after the accident Samuel Walter was taking a nap, but he couldn't sleep and just lay staring. Then, as in a dream, God showed him his son Viktor in an endless fall. Viktor did not seem out of control, but had his arms outstretched as if he were a bird flying through the air.

Samuel knew that this was not an ordinary dream. He called his wife and said, 'Frida, something has happened to Viktor. I saw him falling into a bottomless pit. You must go to Semipalatinsk tomorrow.'

They first prayed together and their prayer confirmed that Viktor was in trouble. Frida bought all manner of nourishing foods, packed her suitcase and took the train to Semipalatinsk, a trip of about fifty hours. After her arrival she first took the road to the base. Outside the gate she miraculously met the only Christian soldier who served together with Viktor, one Vladimir Levardovsky. This Ukrainian soldier told her about the accident. He had already warned the local Christians and he provided Frida with an address where she could get lodgings. Worried, she also visited the hospital but the KGB had left instructions not to allow anyone in to see the convict.

She pleaded and begged, but the doctor was afraid of losing his job and wouldn't allow her in. Frida wept and went to the address the Christian soldier had given her. The people there comforted her and provided her with a place to stay for a few weeks. Regularly she visited the hospital for permission to visit her son. After a few days a nurse managed to motion to Frida to follow her. When they were far enough away from the hospital, the nurse told Frida that she should try approaching the hospital at night. The nurse would help Frida find Viktor's room.

Late that evening Frida visited her son. The nurse had been right: she could slip inside unnoticed. For two weeks she managed to be with her son every night, providing him with good food and tender care. When Frida left for home, the local Christians took over her work, so that Viktor received visits almost every evening after the doctors had gone home.

After six weeks Viktor was discharged. He wasn't sentenced, but had 'invalid' stamped in his military pass. He had been away from home for a total of eighteen months. But God had not approved a seven-year labour camp sentence. Nevertheless, the KGB still considered him an enemy of the state and his dossier would remain active, for perhaps they would need it later on.

For the first two years after the accident Viktor couldn't live without help. It wasn't easy for this strong young man to make the move to a life of total dependence. But he had one consolation: the strange experience during his fall and his father's vision proved that God had a purpose for his illness. Viktor knew with great certainty that even this difficult period would serve the Kingdom of God in one way or another.

As he studied the Bible and was busy in prayer, greater peace and deliberation entered his thoughts. He worried less about his own future, and focused more and more on the future of the congregation.

He asked himself why Christians were so fearful. 'Why do we restrict the Holy Spirit to the welfare of our own individual souls? That can't be the meaning of Pentecost!' Viktor had of course not experienced the terror of Stalin's days himself, but he had heard the stories and could accept that even the thought of it could still paralyse. But this young Christian was driven by an unstoppable desire to test the truth of Scriptures; 'If it's true that the Holy Spirit provides power to endure; . . . if it's true that there is victory for those who are prepared to give their lives on earth; . . . if it's true that Jesus has been given all power in heaven and on earth; . . . if it's true . . .'

Viktor undertook a thorough study of the first Christians. Over and over again his Bible readings surprised him with the courage of people who had opened themselves to the working of the Holy Spirit. He discovered that the miracles and blessings of the first Christians were almost always connected to obedience to God's Word. And he asked himself: 'In view of the fact that Soviet Union Christians always talk about strict obedience to the Word of God, why is it that the Church lives such a fearful and secret life in this country?'

He often discussed these things with his friends and his father. Old Samuel enjoyed those talks about the Bible and the purposes God had for His Church, even though he was anxious about the implications. He was still ashamed of the time in Primorski when he had spiritually abandoned his children. Viktor was right: that must never happen again! But he also was afraid for the future his son would face, as his ideas were sure to bring troubles in their wake. The Bible was so contemporary, and also so radical. 'Don't build your house on sand, but on a rock', Jesus had said. That meant hearing, and doing, the Word. 'Love one another. Love your enemies. Witness with word and deed!'

Of course every believer in the Soviet Union knew what was the right thing to do, but the times were so difficult, and so different than at the time of Jesus. Some even thought that it made no sense any more to preach God to atheists, unbelievers and Muslims. They had long ago written them off, and waited only for Christ's second

coming. But the Bible said, 'He who overcomes and does
My will to the end . . .' Viktor thought a lot about those
words. He knew that his parents, the preachers, and most
other Christians persevered, but only inside their own front
door. They didn't see their faith as relevant to society, or
to their own jobs. Faith only gave personal comfort when
you came in conflict with the authorities, with your boss
and colleagues.

A new thought began to mature inside Viktor: endurance
to the end meant more than keeping your faith. It meant
perseverance in obedience. Perseverance in the Great
Commission. Perseverance in the unity of the Church of
Jesus Christ. He read the words of Jesus in the high-priestly
prayer: 'As you sent Me into the world, I have sent them
into the world' (John 17:18). He understood that the
Church had received this commission to preach the Gospel.
But how had Jesus been sent? And how can we now be sent
like Him? Then he read these words: ' . . . that all of them
may be one, Father, just as You are in Me and I am in You;
may they also be in us so that the world may believe that
you have sent me' (John 17: 21).

Slowly the thought grew that the secret of the victory
does not reside in individual Christians, but in the
congregation, the Church. His own unbridled teenage years
were the consequence of a Church which had lost all
attraction, a Church which no longer took risks to attract
lost souls. Of course, the imprisoned pastors were different.
They were prepared for sacrifices. But as soon as they were
in prison, the congregation collapsed like a house built on
sand.

One question kept haunting Viktor: 'How can a *whole*
congregation, young and old together, become obedient to
God's Word and be united to one purpose?' He simply had
to find that answer. He read how much Jesus and His
disciples fasted and prayed, and he wanted to follow their

example. Then he discovered how much a walk with God through fasting and prayer changed his own life, and his environment too.

After a few years he was able to organize youth activities again, holding prayer services and Bible studies. Without forcing his own ideas, Viktor more and more mentioned that unity would be needed to convince the world of God's love.

From immediate surroundings, but also from farther regions of Central Asia, many young people travelled to Akhangaran to pray together, read the Bible and ponder God's will. They were convinced that a new organization had to be found for Christians to feel less lonely and better prepared to resist the pressures of the authorities.

God was working something brand new. The youth group of the pentecostal assembly of Akhangaran slowly grew into a spiritual laboratory in which work proceeded on a new type of Christian. New for the Soviet Union, that is, for the type had existed already for two thousand years, according to the Scriptures.

6
A New Era

Akhangaran, 1973

The KGB had not remained ignorant of the heightened activities of the pentecostal youth of Central Asia. Viktor Walter, the recuperating youth leader, had been kept under constant observation. A number of times they had threatened him with more gaol, in spite of his illness. The dossier of his refusal to serve in the military was still active. The KGB clerk told him that it contained enough material to get him in front of a judge within two days. Nonchalantly he would add, 'We don't even have to mention your Christian activities, for the psychiatrists have stated that you are not a Christian, but a malingerer.' The agent knew very well that that declaration was false, for in fact they considered him a Christian of the most dangerous kind. Viktor wasn't afraid, and the KGB hated those Christians the most.

There was another reason why Viktor and his dad were under surveillance. Pastor Friesen had fallen seriously ill during his imprisonment, without hope of recovery. In 1971 he had been permitted to go home before the end of his term, and a month later he had been 'promoted to glory'. Would the Akhangaran congregation now fall apart again? Or would the Walters take over leadership? The KGB kept a close eye on developments.

In 1973, three years after his accident, Viktor had to submit to another medical examination. The KGB forced the doctor to conclude that his recovery was complete and that Viktor could return to regular work. Everyone –

including the doctor – knew that he couldn't even tie his own shoe laces, but protests would be useless. The KGB chief was brutal and clear: 'Before your military service time you pretended to be a Christian. To escape your labour camp sentence you threw yourself down from the fifth floor. And now you want to fool us by pretending to be an invalid. You're as lazy as all the other fascists we have already punished for their crimes. Watch your step, otherwise we'll do the same to you.'

Viktor found a job in the railway yards, working for the same foreman as his father. He became a crane operator, which meant that he could sit while working.

Church youth activities continued as before. More and more young friends came to Akhangaran, from far and near. The young people steadily grew together into a solid community, even though the older Christians were still afraid of the KGB. In utmost secrecy they organized small gatherings at out-of-the-way addresses and sheltered open-air spots. More than once such a service had to be cancelled at the last moment, and sometimes weeks went by without meetings.

One day a stranger walked across the yards. From his swinging crane Viktor spotted him. The shabby suit and loud tie advertised him as a KGB agent, a man from around that area. Viktor knew he had to be careful, for locals who worked for the KGB were utterly without scruples, and would do anything for money and power. Samuel Walter saw him too and was scared when he saw the man walk to Viktor's crane. With sad eyes he saw his son slowly creeping out of the cabin and stretching his sore back. Then the man walked him to the waiting car. Father and son exchanged a quick glance. Samuel's nod was meant to convey courage, and Viktor knew that his father had already begun to pray.

The agent took him to the central police station, a superior officer. This man offered Viktor a chair, but the boy wasn't planning on playing his game and remained standing. The KGB agent pretended not to notice and in an artificially sweet voice said, 'Well, Mr Walter, how do you like your new job?' Viktor didn't answer but waited patiently for the reason for this visit. The man was the first to run out of patience. 'Viktor Samuelovich Walter . . .'

Now Viktor was on familiar territory, for this is how each KGB conversation began. Next would be the familiar threats. The KGB man continued, 'You have been regularly attending meetings of the pentecostal church where your father is pastor. And that is not all, for several times you have "preached the Word" there, as you call it. You are aware that we are in a legal position to arrest you, in view of your past. You will remember that we have warned you not to attend the meetings of that congregation any more. Because of our patience, we shall let you go this time, but do not conclude that you can fool us. We know everything about you, literally everything, and about your so-called *brothers* and *sisters*.' He emphasized those last words to indicate his contempt for Christians.

Triumphantly he put his hand on a file on his desk, and listed a number of facts his investigators had gathered. He read the exact times and locations of secret meetings, as well as the contents of the sermons, from the document he waved in Viktor's face. Even the details of the closed meetings of the leaders were known to him.

Viktor pretended not to be impressed and told the man that he had decided long ago to obey God more than men. 'I have warned you', the man said in a threatening tone. He turned around and seated himself behind his desk. 'You may go.'

When Viktor returned home it was dark already. His parents had worried and had been in prayer constantly. He told them the story of the KGB officer. 'They know everything, Dad, even the things only we should have known.' Samuel thought for a while, in an atmosphere of great tension. Then he stood up and said, sighing deeply, 'I think I know what to do, Viktor. We have talked enough about the future of the congregation and I think the moment has come to act. So the KGB knows everything – that's good. They should know everything, for the Kingdom of God is a public matter and the Church of Jesus Christ is not a secret society. That KGB man has given us the solution.

'If he knows everything then it's ridiculous to spend a lot of time travelling to secret places for meetings, and ridiculous to keep our singing soft, and the shutters closed when we study the Bible. From now on we won't hide our activities from anybody any more. Let them come and witness. Perhaps God will witness to their heart.'

Frida came in, and she held her breath as she listened to the words of her husband. Suddenly he looked taller than he actually was, and his eyes sparkled with energy. Their little children peered around the door and the older ones entered one by one. Viktor glowed. He stood up and embraced his Dad. This was a historical moment for the family. Together they knelt down and praised God for His love and the sacrifice of His only Son Who died for the sins of the whole world. As was the custom, everyone prayed aloud a personal prayer, and then silence came. Only Samuel continued in prayer, and while tears were streaming down his face, he said, 'Oh God, help us to obey You. Help us to meet our enemies with the same love Your Son had for His enemies. Amen.'

Viktor could hardly wait to share the news with his youth group and friends. He knew they would respond with enthusiasm. But Samuel faced a more difficult task. At the next service he shared his vision about the congregation's future, telling them that the KGB knew all about them anyway. Full of fear the believers looked around. 'Is there a traitor in our midst?', they asked themselves. 'Probably,' Samuel said bluntly, 'but we'll get rid of him quickly if we free ourselves spiritually. Love will drive away fear. Love is the light which reveals sin. If we do things openly, there is nothing left to be betrayed. So he will either leave or confess his sins.'

Samuel understood that his personal decision would meet strong resistance. These people had already endured so much. They had lost close family and friends in the long battle with the authorities. But now they understood also that even the greatest precautions had been inadequate. The older members wavered between fear and hope. Soon other congregations got to know of Samuel Walter's startling ideas. 'We can't come out in the open without registration,' they said, 'and we can't register for that's against the Scriptures. Samuel and Viktor are too idealistic. It would be nice, but it's a sure way to invite a new wave of hostilities and arrests.'

But while the adults discussed the threats, the youth group was unanimous in its support. Samuel opened his house freely for meetings of the Free Evangelical Christian Church. It had been a long time since a non-registered church had met openly. On hot summer days even the windows were opened, and neighbours and passers-by could enjoy the singing of beautiful hymns. Everyone was welcome. All members were invited to bring along an acquaintance or colleague who expressed interest. The news spread like wildfire through Soviet Central Asia: 'The pentecostals in Akhangaran hold public worship services.'

Of course the meetings also drew the attention of the enemy. But as Samuel had predicted, the KGB was not prepared for this change, and for the moment they had no response to Christians who had overcome their fears.

7
Solid Plans

Akhangaran, 1971–1975

In the meantime, Vladimir Walter had married Anna, the oldest daughter of Wilhelm Friesen. They moved to Merke, three hundred miles east of Akhangaran. Vladimir returned almost every week for consultations, and he wasn't the only one constantly to travel that far. Young Christians regularly came to Akhangaran from all over Central Asia.

Why did they travel those long distances and spend those long hours in buses and trains? The answer was simple: they shared a common goal, for the first time in their lives. They had so much in common: discrimination against them because they were Germans, frustration and resulting alcoholism and violence in their pasts. But God had saved them as out of a fire. Again they met persecution, but now it was because of their faith. Most of them shared the same terrible experiences. But the saddest of all was they had often been alone in their stand. The congregation was not a place you could count on for common resistance.

Viktor and his friends were busy formulating a brand new plan, a plan for everyone, weak and strong, small and big, young and old. It was that plan which brought the friends to Akhangaran all the time. The KGB had been right to suspect that the Walters were up to something. That something was already in the wind, as everyone knew, either friend or foe. The seed had been sown by the martyrs under Stalin and Khrushchev, and it was now busily germinating in this new post-war generation.

Nikolai Vins was one of the friends. He hailed from the mining town of Tabashar, ninety miles south of Akhangaran, a secret source of uranium and therefore not found on many maps. Nikolai's father, being a German, had been forced to work there after the war. After a while his wife Mariya followed him with their two children. On 31st August 1951 Heinrich Vins was taken away and shot, without explanation. Seven months later Nikolai was born.

There were only seven believers in Tabashar, six women and one man. Regularly a few brothers came from Leninabad, the city close by, to lead a secret house church service, and that's how Nikolai had come to the faith in 1969. From then on he regularly joined the youth group in Leninabad, where he met Viktor Walter at a wedding in 1970, and before Viktor's accident. Nikolai had to enter military service shortly after, and later became a congregational youth leader himself before he met Viktor again in 1973.

Gennadi Maydanyuk was another friend, from Tavaksai, a little village about sixty miles west of Akhangaran. Gennadi was the only Russian of that early German pentecostal generation. One day he had invited Viktor and Vladimir to Tavaksai to attend a farewell service before he joined the army. In that small congregation he had been the only young man. After his difficult time in the military he again sought contact with Viktor, and he visited his sick friend, often as many as three times a week.

Bernhard Rosher had also experienced the flight from Cheylabinsk. His parents had escaped into the taiga first, almost to the Sea of Japan, but afterwards had moved to Frunze. Bernhard had been instrumental in the

conversion of Yegor Betcher and his brothers and sisters.
Now he was the pentecostal youth leader in Frunze.

Strong bonds developed between these friends. They
were about the same age and shared a similar spiritual
and social background. But their most important bond
was their desire to serve God. Not one condemned the
earlier Christians who had been reticent under Stalin's
regime. But they were firm in wanting to break through
the vicious circle of servility to atheists. That's why
Viktor's ideas spoke to them. And what attracted them
even more was that those ideas were not Viktor's, but
came directly from the Bible.

Viktor was not even an inspiring speaker – none of
them were, these ordinary workers and common people.
Yet Viktor had something special. His illness had made
him a man of prayer, and when he read the Scriptures,
you knew he had received knowledge straight from God.
When he cited examples from the life of the early
Christian Church, he never sounded theoretical. He
clearly had thought a lot about forming a community
based on Acts 2, and would say, 'Unity is beautiful, but
it must be all-inclusive. In a true community it wouldn't
do to have anyone feel on the outside. If we do something
like it, everyone must be free to come and go. The whole
congregation must bear responsibility for every member,
and every member for the whole of the congregation.
Every rule must be justified by the Bible and must only
be valid for members of the community.'

The plans had to be comprehensive, especially in a
Soviet society where the State had made itself the provider
for the needs of the people. A church that would practise
the principles of the early Christian Church would
inevitably come into conflict with the authorities and the
whole Soviet system.

Viktor had grasped the notion that God does not work

with undue haste. Ideas must have time to mature. They must become so much a part of yourself that you don't feel nervous thinking about them any more, and only then are they ready to be shared. The first careful conversations about forming a community began in 1974.

The friends agreed that there was a great need for a practical Christianity, and they really didn't need any more sermons to inspire them. They were eager to show openly how Christians could live together in accordance with biblical principles. They put it this way: 'Muslims and atheists have to see how Christians live.'

Slowly the ideas of Viktor and his friends gained form. Old Samuel understood that the ideas were not just his son's, but were shared by a whole new generation prepared for sacrifice. But he also worried. Once, alone with Viktor, he said, 'My boy, I thank God for what He is doing in your life and the life of your friends, but I worry. You are an invalid. What will happen to you if they arrest you and lock you up in a concrete cell?' Of course Samuel had a right to worry, for he had indeed experienced Stalin's terror. His own father had been taken away because atheists had spotted an open Bible on his kitchen table, and Samuel never saw him again. Would he now lose his son the same way?

For Viktor Walter, 1975 would be an important year. The friends now met every week. The pentecostal church of Akhangaran was still the only one with open public worship services. More and more people came to listen to the singing and preaching. The Akhangaran Muslims even looked upon them with favour, seeing for the first time Christians who were not afraid of the authorities. Muslims hated the Russian occupiers and they had deep contempt for collaborators.

Viktor and his father were often summoned before the KGB, as were muslim leaders. The KGB kept repeating the same question: 'Will you work along with us?' But neither the faithful Muslims nor the pentecostals were prepared to lift a finger for the KGB. Through these common experiences a bond grew between Samuel and Mullah, the muslim leader. Samuel even began to make mention of the Gospel, and though the man listened attentively, he said, 'Dear friend, we have a different religion. Jesus was a great prophet, the son of Mary and Joseph, but he is not the Son of God.' Yet despite these differences the two remained friends.

However, some Christians accepted the KGB offer and began to feed them information. Sad people, those. Even if their work was hidden for a long time in congregations in which spiritual gifts were at a low ebb, sooner or later they were discovered. Afterwards no congregation would have them any more. The KGB also had no further use for them and discarded them like rubbish.

By contrast, spiritual gifts were many and rich in the church of Akhangaran which had opened its doors wide for anyone. Young people freely prayed, and God regularly spoke directly through visions and prophecies. In such a church no KGB helpers could infiltrate, for they would be unmasked almost immediately.

A brother arrived all the way from Riga, capital of Latvia, and brought with him his extraordinary gift. He spoke simply about practical effects of the Word of God. For instance, he cited James 5 for the case of illness, where elders are called and anoint with oil. 'Jesus is as powerful now as he was then', this Latvian evangelist said.

Viktor listened with rapt attention. This man read the Bible the same way as he did. At the end of his sermon the speaker asked who of them desired to be prayed over. Viktor was the first to give voice to his needs. Everyone knelt down and the brother from Riga came to stand next to Viktor. He rubbed some oil in his hands and put them on Viktor's head. Immediately the young man began to glow with heat, as if an electric current went through his whole body. After the prayer he felt supple and discovered that all pain had left him. The congregation broke out in celebration that day, for after five years Viktor had regained his full health. A few days afterwards he helped move a piano from the third floor.

That same year Viktor Walter married Mariya Pavlovets, a young woman originally from White Russia. To their wedding came many friends, from White Russia and Central Asia. But it wasn't only a time of feasting: meetings were held to make plans. Viktor and Mariya had spoken often about the possibility of forming a community with other Christians. They both were prepared to give their own marriage and family second place, realizing that a fellowship could only thrive if leaders sacrificed their own interests. At the wedding ceremony Viktor stated that the needs of the Church of Jesus Christ would have priority over his own marriage, and Mariya promised that she would not demand that her husband pay more attention to her than to the needs of the congregation.

These words became the spur for their friends to make firm plans for a new communal lifestyle. One of them suggested a return to Primorski, an idea that appealed to all those who had lived there before. They had changed, and now they sensed the need to do mission work among the godless population of that far away province near the Sea of Japan.

'If we do it, we should operate as a congregation there, for there are no churches in Primorski', someone said. Yet that wasn't something they had considered before, for they were already members of a congregation, and none of them seemed old and experienced enough to lead a church.

These Akhangaran young people had already received a lot of criticism from older Christians. Viktor now received his full share from the Germans for marrying a Russian woman, but his parents supported him. Like other young people he and Mariya felt that a born-again Christian had no time for nationalist passions and discrimination. But now that these embittered older people heard about the concrete plans for a new congregation, new criticism burst over those young heads.

The Soviet Central Asian young Christians, and in particular those of Akhangaran, had only one goal: to use existing congregations for a religious revival in the Soviet Union. Much prayer and fasting helped establish a climate of anticipation. God heard their prayers. New life had begun and the first signs of revival were obvious.

Having heard all the criticism and experienced the opposition, they decided to get objective advice from some wise brothers. Alas, these were far away, for in Central Asia only opposition could be found to their plans. Viktor travelled to the Ukraine and to White Russia, where he had heard that gifts of prophecy and revelation flourished. No money was available to send more people, and few could take enough time off work anyway. Fortunately Viktor could, for he worked the same crane as his father, who promised to take his shifts. Viktor wanted the answers to three key questions:

1. Would they have to form a church as part of a community?
2. Where should they establish it?
3. Who should become the new community's pastor?

Viktor's first stop was the pentecostal congregation of Pinsk. It took him a week to travel the thousands of miles. They received him warmly and he immediately visited a man known to be a prophet. But instead of posing the questions first, Viktor asked him to pray for a revelation from God. It would be clearer that God would be speaking if the man didn't already know the circumstances.

Even that first evening the prophet made clear that God approved the plans for a new congregation. But he revealed much more. Viktor heard that they could expect a time of great difficulty. 'You will have to go barefoot through a bed of coals', the prophet said.

The next day Viktor travelled to Rovno, a few hours to the south. The pastor there brought him to another brother known to be a prophet. Viktor did not provide him with details either, but asked the brother to pray for a revelation of God. He heard the same things as in Pinsk, plus a warning that he himself would have to travel a road of suffering.

From Rovno Viktor travelled sixty miles south towards the Romanian border, to the pentecostal congregation of Vinnitsa, where a third prophet gave him the same message, indeed in literally the same words as in the two previous locations. He carefully recorded the three prophecies in writing on his way back to Akhangaran.

From these three prophecies at least one piece of advice was clear: *Your plans are good, but stay in Central Asia for the moment, until you are strong enough and have consolidated your unity. Only then shall I send you to a place you want to go yourself. There you shall endure severe persecution for My Name's sake. I shall guide your feet through fire and test your walk of life. Your pastor will be imprisoned. After a period of persecution I shall lead you out. I shall make of you a large congregation in which My Name shall be glorified.*

The answers to their questions left no doubt. They were given permission to begin a community and a congregation. But they had to postpone their desire to move to Primorski.

They realized the seriousness of these prophecies: they could expect persecution. Yet their heart was set on obeying God.

And so the end of 1975 marked the beginning of a new congregation after the model of the first Christians as described in the book of Acts.

8
A Community of Love
Akhangaran, 1976

A month of much prayer and fasting followed Viktor's strategic travels. God had put His stamp of approval on the plans to establish a new congregation after the blueprint of the first Christians, and the real work could only begin now. Making use of a few holidays in early 1976, all the friends came together in Akhangaran, this time for the specific purpose of establishing clear guidelines. Not only specifically church matters, but daily routines (marriage, raising children, finances, housing, jobs, training, etc.) had to be considered. Moreover, the structure of leadership needed to be firmly established.

During the meeting the participants fasted strictly and prayed much. God was so near to them. He instructed the brothers on all matters that were held up to Him in prayer. Gradually a grand pattern emerged, a mosaic of all the necessary rules to which the Word of God guided them. The participants lost all sense of time, for these were holy hours. After about fifteen hours, they took stock. To almost all questions a biblical answer had been discovered, and 'The Regulations for the Free Evangelical Christian Church' charter was established. Even today these regulations are strictly followed, not as a set of choking conditions but as a point of rest needed to ensure peace and harmony in God's family.

The goal of the new congregation was captured in these two points:

1. Preach the Gospel.
2. Live a practical Christianity.

This new community intended to show Akhangaran what it really meant to be a Christian in daily life. Almost half the twenty-two regulations mentioned in the charter pertained to social and economic matters, each with their specific biblical references. Consider regulation three, for instance, an example of how the new community combined spiritual and practical aspects.

When a person turns towards God, he must, with all his heart and without reservation, alter his opinions, objectives, desires and his entire life (2 Corinthians 5:17; Romans 6:4).

If before he went his own way and did what was right in his own eyes, he must now live for God and His will alone (1 Peter 4:1–3; 2 Corinthians 5:15; Ephesians 4:23).

It signifies that every member no longer claims ownership over anything, but considers all things the property of the Congregation. (Acts 2:44–45; 4:32)

Their attention to suffering was typical of these young brothers, who really knew what it was like to be persecuted for the faith. Here is the sixth regulation:

The person who turns to God must realize that he will enter the 'narrow road', the path which leads to persecution for the Name of Jesus Christ, the road to suffering and great pain (Matthew 7:13–14; 5:10, 11; John 15:18–20; Matthew 24:9; Mark 13:9; John 16:33; 17:14; Hebrews 13:13–15; Acts 14:22; 1 Corinthians 4:9–13; 2 Corinthians 6:4–10; 11:22–29; 12:10; Philippians 1:29–30; 1 Thessalonians 3:3–4; 2 Timothy 2:3; 3:11, 12; Revelation 6:9–11; 7: 13, 14)

During the same day of fasting the difficult subject of leadership was raised. The structures had been agreed upon, but a pastor had to be chosen, and the regulations stated: 'The pastor will be elected by the whole congregation.' For Viktor the choice was clear: his father, old Samuel. But the Lord Himself revealed that Viktor was to be that person. Viktor felt himself unworthy for the difficult post, but he did not wish to be disobedient, and so he became the choice of the congregation. That meant that he also became the head of the entire community.

This extraordinary meeting had drastic consequences. A number of houses had to be constructed quickly, for soon several additional families would move to Akhangaran. They quickly learned to build the loam houses typical of that region. They used their bare hands to mix mud and straw, and baked the bricks in the sun. Before too long they reached a production rate of 1500 bricks per day, a quantity that made even skilled brick-makers take notice. It wasn't difficult to see how that could happen, for even from a distance you could hear the singing and laughter while everyone steadily worked at a good pace. Even the immediate neighbours took pleasure in that group of young men and women who were labouring with so much enthusiasm. Soon good relations developed, which of course enabled the newcomers to speak about their faith. Those muslim neighbours politely listened and seemed interested, but as soon as they sensed that a response was required to the Gospel, they graciously thanked them for the conversation and resumed their own routines.

In those days most of the members found jobs and shelter, and that first year the community lived the way it had imagined.

Soon after construction of the first few houses, Russian pentecostal leaders (called bishops) came to visit Akhangaran. Rumours had reached them, of course, and they came to discover the facts for themselves. Most of them were men of experience and sound spiritual direction.

Actually, they had expected to find strange doctrines among these young people, but they soon discovered that everything they saw and heard was scriptural. Of course they had to get used to the lifestyle, but when they read the regulations they responded, 'This is according to the Scriptures. Time will tell whether it will work in practice, but we give you our blessing.'

Paul Stubert from Dzhalalabad, a city on the borders of Kirgizia and Uzbekistan, was especially helpful. This lonely battler deeply enjoyed the mission activities of this young congregation. He frequently invited Viktor and the others to accompany him to faraway villages, where often he knew a solitary Christian living among the Muslim. Sometimes even unbelievers and Muslims warmly welcomed them into their homes to hear the Gospel. More than once a small meeting was organized where people sang and enjoyed a practical Bible study. Paul Stubert was a real evangelist and shepherd of souls. He loved people and knew instinctively when someone needed spiritual or practical assistance.

The Akhangaran congregation was not wealthy. Most of the members had arrived with only a few small suitcases. But now that they all lived together, they experienced how efficient the first Christian community must have been. They undertook everything communally, including paying jobs. Group contracts with employers made it possible for small mission teams to use a few days for visits to more distant regions.

Beside evangelism, they also extended material assistance outside the congregation. Some members cared for the vegetable garden of an old, sick woman; others did the household work for a mother of a large family, whose husband only came home to sober up; an aged man whose pension was inadequate received clothing and extra food.

During those first few years the members got to know each other's gifts and characteristics. One member was a good gardener, another a skilled housekeeper, a third an excellent mechanic. 'Specialists' for congregational work also emerged: a choir director, an organizer of special celebrations, leaders for youth and children, etc. Viktor knew that everyone had to be prepared to do everything, but he also understood that the work a person enjoys most honours God most in the end.

One of the congregation's favourite verses was James 2:18: 'But someone will say, "You have faith; I have deeds." Show me your faith without deeds, and I will show you my faith by what I do.'

In their immediate surroundings there were many opportunities to show faith by works. Colleagues and neighbours soon got to know that Christians lived near. Fortunately few problems resulted.

If there was a problem, Old Russians caused them, indoctrinated as they were in atheism and affected by the war. They seemed to have a hard time reacting normally, especially when they spotted these young folk singing on the street or on the bus. They would yell the most horrible things – 'Shoot them.' 'Why don't they lock them up?'

The Akhangaran 'missionaries' did not let themselves be provoked into an argument. If they weren't welcome, they simply moved on or held their tongues. They only looked for positive opportunities to share the love of God. Some of the traditions they had picked up from their families helped them do just that. For instance, no matter where they ate, in public places too, they would first stand up and pray. Nobody interfered with them, even though some people would look startled. Sometimes people would ask them why they did that, and then those young people would simply tell them that no food is to be taken for granted. 'Having enough to eat is a gift of God and that's why we thank Him.' Every Soviet citizen could understand that, for most of them had experienced shortages and hunger.

Soviet citizens publicly read in the strangest places, even on escalators leading to the underground. Those young Akhangaran Christians were avid readers too, predominantly of the New Testament, and of the whole Bible if they were rich enough to have one. Few people had seen such a small yet bulky book, and often a good talk with fellow passengers about the Bible and God's plan were the result.

Hours of bus rides would be required for small groups to visit small villages. One of them would ask the driver's permission for some singing, which was often readily given, for singing helped enliven the long, monotonous ride. The other passengers would listen attentively and after a few hymns most of the bus would be filled with conversations about faith. Sometimes a committed atheist would object, and then these young evangelists would stop immediately. They held on to their motto never to preach in an unfriendly and inhospitable atmosphere, but simply to lead a Christian life.

Teams of them also travelled to towns in Central Asia where they had lived before, for instance to Tabashar, the former home of Nikolai Vins. His brother Johan still lived there, but he and his wife Ella didn't want to hear about faith at first. Johan especially lived an unbridled life. He drank too much and often abused his wife and their three small children. However, when Nikolai and members of the team visited them, both Johan and Ella listened attentively to the enthusiastic stories from Akhangaran. Johan became intrigued and wanted to know more, about God and about the problems of his own lifestyle. He realized he was on a wrong road, and he remembered his own mother's very different teaching. After a number of conversations he came to realize how much he needed God, as much as his brother Nikolai did, and he knelt down to confess his sins.

An older couple from Tabash, Christian and Nelie Stumpf, had also been brought up as Christians, but now they lived secular lives, and their children were members of communist youth groups. The evangelists told them about Jesus. The patience and love they exuded were a very new experience for hotheaded Christian. He was full of questions, but after a few meetings he embraced the faith. His children too were converted and resigned from the communist youth groups. But Nelie held out, even though Christians now entered her house regularly for meetings. Her conversion took place much later.

In Tabashar the group was invited to lead a funeral. They turned it into a very special evangelism meeting, witnessing to the death and resurrection of Jesus Christ, and singing hymns which deeply touched the hearts of many people. Their words were honest and straightforward. Those people in Tabashar heard that God knew their doubts and fears of death, subjects that were never raised in that city. Yet most of the men who worked in the uranium mine would die before they were fifty. They listened, quietly and with full attention. What they heard was very new, very different. How could people so young be so sure?

Most conversions took place within circles of friends, and few occurred as a result of street preaching. Yet one feared hothead came to Christ just like that. He radically turned his life around and joined the Akhangaran community. (Alas, after some time he turned away from the narrow road, even though he still went to other worship services.) Yet the meagre harvest gathered through evangelism on buses, trains and in public places gave these young Christians no cause to work any other way. They were convinced that obedience to Christ's commission to go out into the whole world was more important than tangible results. They knew that God has a road for each human being, and that every child of God must function as a road sign.

Lyudmila Teplikh had not received any Christian nurture. Her father, a former criminal, had become a Christian in gaol through a fellow prisoner who was a Baptist minister. Lyudmila's mother wanted nothing to do with her husband's new faith, even though the children now went to church with their father. Lyudmila became a nurse and went to work in the Tabashar hospital. Away from the father's hold over her, she stopped going to church. She believed in her own way, kneeling in prayer only when she was in trouble.

And did she get in trouble! Everyone who could be spared had to help with the cotton harvest: children and workers who could leave their regular jobs, even nurses. With some discipline, it could have been an interesting break, but cotton harvest was known for its lawlessness, a place not suited for a twenty-year-old girl! Lyudmila prayed to God: 'Lord God, if You are there, protect me during cotton harvest so that no one will touch me. If You do that, I'll serve You always.'

Her prayer was heard. God did protect her, and afterwards she wanted to live up to her promises. She went looking for Christians so that she could join a church. Shortly after, she saw a patient her own age copying hymns into a notebook. Lyudmila recognized some of them and asked the girl why she was doing that. 'An old grandma asked me to do that', she said casually. Actually, it had been her own mother, a member of the pentecostal congregation, but she was ashamed to admit it. The nurse asked her to introduce her to that 'old grandma'. The girl hadn't counted on that and asked her mother for the address of an old woman. She gave it to Lyudmila who soon after took up contact with the old woman who belonged to the Tabashar pentecostal congregation, and who warmly invited her to attend a service.

The next Sunday she attended a service where Christian Stumpf was the preacher. He told her that there were many young people of her age in his own Akhangaran congregation. The next week the nurse took the first bus to Akhangaran, where she soon found friends in a vibrant congregation. There she professed her faith and faithfully followed Bible study sessions. Subsequently she often took the four-hour bus ride back and forth.

When the head of her department found out that Lyudmila had become a Christian, he tried everything in his power to change her mind. He got all kinds of library books to prove that faith is superstition and that the Bible is unscientific. Lyudmila wasn't very receptive to these well trodden paths of atheist propaganda. Finally, her boss asked her, with penetrating eyes, 'Lyudmila, have you perhaps been baptized with the Holy Spirit?' 'Yes', she said boldly. The man was startled and said, 'No wonder I can't change your mind. It says in this book that talks about this subject have no effect on people who have been baptized with the Holy Spirit.'

On 14th June 1980 Lyudmila was baptized in Akhangaran, where she now took up residence too. Her 'concerned' boss had not been willing to give her a day off, and so she resigned. Much prayer had led her to that decision.

The KGB was inundated with reports about the evangelistic activities of this pentecostal community. In a short time six other small congregations had been founded. The young evangelists were on the road almost daily to visit these groups, as well as solitary Christians. They celebrated communion, conducted Bible studies, and held evangelistic services.

It was most often Samuel Walter whom the KGB called

to task. He got to hear a variety of complaints about the behaviour of 'his youth'. He was threatened with the arrest of Viktor and the other leaders. Actually, the KGB didn't realize that Viktor was the pastor, presuming the oldest member to have that function, as with the Muslims. Samuel never did set them straight, thinking: 'Let them think that, then Viktor remains out of danger.'

When it became clear that neither talks nor threats would work, they tried infiltrators who would pretend to be Christians, often criminals with a tragic past. They would tell of dramatic conversions and request membership in the congregation. But the community would ask for confirmation by the Spirit, Who would always speak clearly through prophecies and visions, and so unmask the infiltrators.

The revelations in the Akhangaran congregation came to influence other Central Asian congregations. They had to acknowledge that God protected these young people in a most remarkable way. They themselves had often harboured traitors for many years and had experienced much trouble because of them. In Akhangaran, however, these vile wretches had no chance at all.

9
The New Mission Field

Primorski, 1981

The items in the 'Walter Case' dossier grew more numerous . . . as did the number of Christians. Alarming bits of information reached KGB headquarters from all over Central Asia. Frequent summoning of Samuel Walter, many threats, constant observations of Viktor — nothing had any effect. Christians who kept themselves in the background before were now listed as prime suspects. And the Akhangaran community kept attracting 'problems', people like Yegor Betcher who had turned a whole barracks upside down with his miracle healing, and agitators Bernhard Rosher and Nikolai Vins, both pentecostal youth leaders. Yet it wasn't so easy to accuse the congregation of activity against the state. Many citizens admired the manner in which these Christians cared not only for themselves but for people outside the congregation too. Even the mullah, the leader of all faithful Muslims, supported them, and the KGB could not ignore his opinion.

The only option these 'protectors of marxist ideology' had was to destroy the cause of all this unrest: Viktor Walter! 'If we arrest him, the whole sect will collapse like a house of cards.'

In the meantime, God put before the Akhangaran brothers ever more clearly the task of expanding their missionary efforts. The six small pentecostal congregations in Central Asia functioned quite well on their own by now. The prophecies from White Russia and the Ukraine left no room for doubt: Central Asia was only a beginning. A task awaited them in the Far East.

No one could ignore the signals. KGB pressure and the threat of arrest was one. The most important signal, however, was the growing desire to return to Primorski. The ones who had lived there before talked about it more and more. 'If you have once lived in that wild green world you can never get used to the hot and dusty desert of Central Asia', they kept saying.

In late 1980 the congregation decided to explore the possibilities, so in January 1981, Viktor Walter, accompanied by his brother Vladimir, Yegor Betcher and Anatoli Khokha, took a plane to the far east. They travelled over ragged mountains, endless steppes and taigas, everything covered with a thick layer of snow and ice. The flight to Vladivostok, the largest Soviet harbour on the Sea of Japan, took eight hours. From the airport they took a bus straight north. During that two-hour trip they rehearsed the essential points once more: houses not too expensive; enough jobs; reasonably close to shops and schools; good roads.

They got off the bus in Ussurisk, the second largest city in Primorski. It was already dark, and they decided to find a hotel for the night. The next morning they set out to investigate. They soon discovered that house prices were too high here, so they travelled on to Arsenev, ninety miles to the east. The land grew in beauty as they travelled, across the Arsenyevka river and through a beautiful area full of snow-covered hills. They saw extensive forests, pretty rivers and picturesque villages. When they talked, they revived memories, and all four of them thought: 'We're home again!'

In Akhangaran the decision had already been taken to separate into two groups, and find three Primorski locations for settlement. Thus, Yegor and Anatoli continued on their own to Warfolomeyevka, the town of their youth. When they left the train the freezing air cut off their breath, but it also made them think back to their past. They recognized the clear clean air of the region. Nothing much had changed. However, with pain Yegor noticed the many cleared spots in the taiga, for lumber exports to Japan were slowly changing Primorski into a barren land.

Houses were considerably cheaper in Warfolomeyevka, but they wanted to travel even further east. They took the train to the end of the line, Chuguyevka. Houses were affordable here too, and there were plenty of jobs. But they were after three locations, so they also visited Kavalerovo, another sixty miles to the east. Viktor and Vladimir continued their scouting in Arsenyev and Ussurisk. Jobs were plentiful everywhere, but when the foursome got together again, they all felt that Warfolomeyevka and Chuguyevka were the preferred locations, and they decided that these two towns would serve as initial mission posts.

Viktor and Vladimir returned to Akhangaran to consult with the congregation. Yegor stayed in Warfolomeyevka and Anatoli in Chuguyevka, both to find suitable lodging and to apply for residency and work permits, so as to promote speedy settlement. They promised to report their progress by telegram.

On the Arsenyev station platform they said goodbye, praying together that God would protect them and point them to the right settlement locations. Vladimir was already inside the train, but Viktor still hesitated and then said, his face serious: 'Yegor, Anatoli, don't separate. Search for one location together. God will lead you.' The train was moving, but Viktor took Vladimir's hand and jumped on just in time.

The two scouts were on their own, happy about the last-minute decision. Without saying it, they had worried about being separated. It was dark, and time to find a place to stay for the night. Yegor remembered a girl he had known as a teenager, who now lived in Arsenyev. He hadn't seen her for ten years, but since he knew no one else there, they set out to find her. Fortunately, Lyuba was home, and after Yegor shouted his name through the locked door, they were warmly invited in. Of course Lubya was curious about the reason for Yegor's visit, but after he and Anatoli told their story, she grew silent. The story of Yegor's conversion impressed her deeply, and she needed time to think about it.

The next morning the two pioneers left for Warfolomeyevka, where they had the address of two elderly Christians who lived just outside the town. Close to the house they spotted the old man in his yard filling a sack with coal. Anatoli approached and showed him a piece of paper bearing the man's name and address.

'Yes, that's me', the old man said, looking suspiciously at the two strangers through his crooked glasses. 'Are you Christians?' 'Yes, and we would dearly love to talk with you', said Anatoli, while Yegor picked up the heavy sack of coal and carried it into the house. Soon they were sitting in the cosy kitchen and telling the man the reason for their visit. 'Actually, I don't know any believers around here', said the old man, shuffling to the stove to pour hot water into the tea pot. 'But I know a woman in Arsenyev and she has regular contact with other Christians. Why don't you stay here for the night and find her tomorrow.'

After a good night's sleep they took the first train back to Arsenyev. If they had not been short of time, they would have walked the twelve miles through the forests. Everything was white with snow now, but soon spring would come. Who would forget spring in Primorski, a virtual explosion of light and life? In this part of the world nature only has a few months to germinate and blossom, and all that is alive seems to want to make up for lost time in a hurry.

When the two young men arrived at the Arsenyev address, they discovered that a worship meeting had been planned for that day. With what seemed like reverence the old woman said, 'Brother Ivan Mosgovoy will be here, our elder.'

A few hours later Yegor and Anatoli found themselves guests of eight sweet grandmas, each one surprised to see these two young men who had come from so far. When Ivan Mosgovoy entered, Yegor and Anatoli stood up and bowed before the pastor, following the example of the women. Ivan was a simple man who had lived and worked in Arsenyev for many years, where he spent his free time encouraging lonely Christians and strengthening them. He had seldom encountered young Christians.

'Are you believers?' he asked the two guests, observing them carefully. 'Yes', they replied in unison. 'Splendid, then let's pray together.' He immediately knelt down, and everyone else did the same. The Akhangaran men sensed right away that Ivan Mosgovoy was a remarkable man, for during this hour of prayer they forgot this room full of old people. These were missionary prayers, for the coming of a young congregation, and these people were close to the fulfilment of their prayers without even realizing it. Yegor and Anatoli prayed aloud too and the Spirit of God entered, for one of the grandmas received a prophecy: 'Thus speaks the Lord,' she said solemnly, 'these are my children who will live here to work for Me.'

As was the custom, prayers ended with the Lord's Prayer. Then they had a celebration together. The old women were filled with joy. Ivan too was glad to hear that God was sending people to this demanding mission field. Yegor and Anatoli told the story of their Akhangaran community, and revealed their plans to begin work in Warfolomeyevka and Chuguyevka. 'I know someone who lives just outside Chuguyevka,' Ivan said, 'Tatyana

Sheudkova, a woman who has suffered much and who is on her own as a believer. I think she'll be pleased to provide you with lodging. She lives in the suburb of Sokolovka.'

They took the train east once more, and then, after arriving in Chuguyevka, took the city bus to Sokolovka. Tatyana was home, but barely opened the door on seeing these two strange men. However, when she heard the name of Ivan Mosgovoy she warmly welcomed them into her home. Yegor and Anatoli told her the reason for their visit and Tatyana replied: 'You can stay here until you have found a home.' That day, on 10th February 1981, they wired to Akhangaran: 'We're in Chuguyevka and will buy a house if you approve.'

While Tatyana prepared dinner, Tolya Sheludkov, her son, entered, for the most important evening of his life. He made two new friends, yes, but more importantly, this prodigal son returned to his Father.

Within a week the two scouts found an old house on the river. Having suffered fire damage, it was available for very little money. It took some ten days for the return message from Akhangaran, but on 20th February the deal was made and preparations started to receive the first family.

Akhangaran, February 1981

Tensions had increased markedly. The KGB had got wind of the congregational plans to move. Their 'honour' wouldn't let them allow the Walters to leave just like that, so they decided to arrest Viktor. During a prayer meeting the Holy Spirit made clear that danger threatened, so the decision was taken to send Viktor first, instead of last, as the intention had originally been.

Vladimir Walter still lived in Merke, because his wife Anna, Wilhelm Friesen's daughter, felt reluctant to join the community. Viktor, Mariya and their four children immediately took a car to Merke, which was on the route to the far east. In the meantime, Yakov Dik bought enough train tickets from Akhangaran to Chuguyevka, the plan being to change places with the Walters in Merke.

Viktor hadn't been gone more than thirty minutes before a number of police jeeps stopped in front of his house, with a warrant for his arrest. When they learned where he had gone, they sped to the station. Yakov and Irena Dik sat in the train, saw the police, and heard from other travellers that 'a dangerous man' was supposed to be on the train. The train slowly pulled out of the station and a thorough search of it was undertaken. Yakov and Irena sat quietly in constant prayer. The police entered their compartment too, inspected their ticket, even involved a superior officer, but realized that they had been too late. At the next station they all left the train. And in Merke Viktor and his family took their places.

On 4th March 1981, after eight days, they arrived in Chuguyevka, where they met Anatoli and Yegor. The temperature was forty below, and they longed for a warm house and a long sleep. But when they reached the house, after ploughing through thick snow, they were dismayed: it was dirty and cold, and everything was still black from the fire. The two pioneers had cleaned it up a bit, but it wasn't suitable for a family with small children. They got the kitchen stove going full blast and stuffed old rags in the cracks in the wall. The first night they all slept in the kitchen. Yet, in spite of these problems, they felt secure in the knowledge that God had led them to this place.

By the time Mariya and the children woke up the next morning, Viktor had already walked around outside. He was full of enthusiasm and said, 'God has meant this place to be ours, for in the field next door we will build other houses.' But first they purchased a number of existing old houses for the families already on their way.

Soon afterwards, most of the other families and some single people arrived. They had already learned that comfort was less important than being and working together.

Gennadi Maydanyuk, Bernhard Rosher and Johan Vins stayed behind longest to sell the community houses and other belongings. It took them another year to move. Vladimir Walter also stayed another year. Just before he left for a visit to Chuguyevka his wife suggested, 'Why don't you take two of the children, they'll like the trip.' A week after his departure she sent him a telegram: 'Dear Vladimir, hurry back alone to sell the house. We're all going to Chuguyevka.' After that she dropped all her reservations and became a faithful community member.

A month after the arrival of the first family, the pioneers received a permit to build on the river property next to the old house. The air was filled with sawing and hammering. Conditions and materials were very different from those in Central Asia, but the project progressed well. Tolya Sheludkov was skilled in the construction of frame houses, and God had guided matters so that he could teach the newcomers the tricks of the trade.

The history of the Free Evangelical Christian Church had entered a new stage with the establishment of the 'Chuguyevka Congregation'.

10
The Firstfruits

The whole neighbourhood was astonished at the rapid and
accomplished way in which the newcomers built their
houses. Most remarkably, they did everything
collaboratively. Women and girls undertook most of the
finishing work: plastering, hanging wall paper, painting,
cleaning and arranging the furniture. The men could only
build in their spare time, for they had found paid jobs
almost immediately. Just as in Akhangaran, they tried to
work in teams for the same employer, for then the building
of houses and impending evangelism could always be
ongoing.

Making money was no problem in Primorski, and the
wages were a bit higher here. The Walters could continue
their trade as crane operators, while others worked in the
taiga as forestry workers. But their improved living
conditions did not make them forget their purpose for
moving. Building personal careers and luxury houses didn't
enter their thoughts. A simple dwelling was sufficient, as
long as it was warm enough to protect them against the
bitter winter blasts. During that first summer, shelter had
to be provided for a hundred and fifty men, women and
children.

By the end of April the first cars and motor cycles arrived
by train, packed in large crates. The time had come to
reconnoitre the territory. Ivan Mosgovoy the old missionary
pioneer from Arsenyev accompanied them. Viktor and Ivan
had become good friends at first sight.

When Labour Day came (1st May), Viktor, Nikolai Vins and Ivan used the few days off from work to travel towards the Sea of Japan. Nikolai saw for the first time the impressive beauty of this part of the Soviet Union. They took the 'A181', the only road connection with the east, an impressive line on the map but in reality an unpaved road with deep holes and muddy sections. From the Ussuri valley this road crawled upwards towards the seven hundred and fifty miles of the Sikhotelinski mountain range which divides Primorski in two from north to south.

For hours they travelled through the forests. The summit was still covered by a pack of snow. Now and then they passed valleys where not one tree was left standing – they had already learned of the disastrous trade agreement with Japan which annually cost this region three to four million of the most beautiful trees in the world. Tolya Sheludkov was often heard to grumble about this destruction of nature: 'Those atheists are crazy. God won't give His blessing on this destructive work. His creation is groaning.'

Six hours into the trip the trees began to show a strange and unnatural colour, the result of a large chemical factory in Dalnyegorsk, their destination.

In Dalnyegorsk Ivan knew an old Christian woman, who was happily surprised to see the old pastor and his friends. Quickly she invited neighbours and friends in, and that evening they held their first evangelistic service. Full of attention, the small group listened to the songs, a short Bible study, and testimonies by Viktor and Nikolai. It all sounded so real, so alive to them. These young men of not yet thirty loved God, and their talk was so different from other men of their age. People in Primorski had grown so coarse, with curses and obscenities part of almost every sentence. Enthralled, they listened to these young missionaries from Central Asia. Everyone wanted to learn more about the Bible, and they at once scheduled a second meeting.

On the trip back Viktor said, 'Brothers, I am convinced that we have already started a second congregation. From now on we'll arrange for some members to visit Dalnyegorsk every week for worship services.' Ivan's heart overflowed with joy. All his life he had worked on his own, and now a whole young congregation stood behind the mission work.

This veteran evangelist knew that some other Christians lived in the nearby village of Kavalerovo, the former residence of the Rosher family. Here too a missionary outpost was quickly established. They looked not only towards the east, but in all directions for suitable locations for missionary work.

At first these new sister congregations consisted of Christians who had not been members of a church before. The first task for the Chuguyevka congregation was to establish a functional structure for them: a worship service every Sunday, Bible study and prayer meetings during the week. It was also important that provision be made for the sacrament, especially communion.

The construction of houses showed steady progress. The work of the community made a deep impression on Tolya Sheludkov. He wanted to spend all his time with them, but he had Olga and his two children to care for. Sometimes his new friends tried to remind him, but almost immediately Tolya's anger would stand in the way of calm discussion. Only Viktor Walter seemed able to take with the recently converted Tolya. The pastor didn't press any issue, but would only say: 'Tolya, when the Bible speaks to you specifically, try to obey the Word that same day. When you do that, God will change your life more and more.' Viktor's wise counsel and patience helped Tolya a lot. Past fears and frustrations had made him uncertain, but as he read his Bible more and more, and acted on what it instructed him to do, his spiritual confidence grew and his life changed visibly. Even Olga noticed how her husband grew more peaceful and less aggressive every day. She joined him for church services once in a while. When her unbelieving friends and neighbours asked her why she bothered with 'those Christians' she would answer, 'This beats living with a drunkard. Nobody could change Tolya before, but since the Christians came I can't believe what my eyes see.'

While busy on the housing project one day, Tolya saw a stranger approaching. The man went straight to Tolya and without even asking him his name, said, 'Sheludkov, report to Captain Tulnov'.

Tulnov! Tolya knew who he was, a member of the criminal investigation department. Tolya turned towards Viktor Walter who stood close by. Viktor nodded reassuringly, as if to say, 'Don't be afraid, we'll pray for you.'

Tolya suspected why the KGB wanted to see him. He wasn't afraid of them, but he feared himself more, feared losing his temper. When he arrived at the station, Tulnov wasn't even there, but two strange men in plain clothes were waiting. One introduced himself as lieutenant-colonel Bykov, head of the KGB in Primorski. The other, a KGB agent from Chuguyevka, locked the door behind Tolya.

'Sit down', Bykov said in an accommodating tone. 'Perhaps you understand why we have called you?'

Tolya knew very well. It wouldn't be difficult to manufacture an accusation against him, which they would then use to blackmail him into providing information about the Christians.

'You want me to work for you', he said coolly.

'Exactly. You've got it right. But why use that tone of voice? Is it so bad to work for us. Our work is useful: fighting against capitalism.'

While Tolya contemplated those remarks, something miraculous took place. Instead of hate, he only felt pity for those two well dressed gentlemen. Calmly he said, 'I've come to know God and I won't work for you. By the way, why do you have a Russian Bible from Canada in your pocket?'

Bykov was amazed. How could this forest worker know exactly what he had in his pocket? But the KGB officer quickly regained his composure, produced the Bible from his pocket and, pretending not to have caught the remark, opened it at the location of a bookmark.

'This book in which you believe, Anatoli Leonidovich, tells me something important. Listen carefully: " . . . There is no authority except that which God has established. The authorities that exist have been established by God. Consequently, he who rebels against the authority is rebelling against what God has instituted, and those who do so will bring judgement onto themselves."'

Tolya had read that part of Romans the week before. He also remembered that he had read another chapter of Romans, in which he was told that no authority, not even angels, could separate him from the love of Christ.

Viktor had taught Tolya not to enter into debates with unbelievers, so he replied, 'Your explanation of that passage is wrong. I know who you are, even though you don't wear a uniform. Blood soils your hands. I don't want to discuss anything with you.'

When they saw that their plan had failed, they let him go. On his way home Tolya thanked God for the words He had given him, proof that God would never abandon him. The incident also made him realize that he had friends who would continue to pray for him.

Olga Sheludkova was happy about the changes in her husband, but jealous at the same time. She didn't think it right that she, who had borne the brunt of all the misery her husband heaped upon her, now received hardly any attention from him. He was too busy with his new friends, and hardly came home any more, just as had happened in his drinking days.

One morning, when Tolya had already left, and Olga was still in bed, resting with little Svetlana, there came up from the cellar a noise that sounded like the gnawing of rats. They had been bothered by these rodents lately and Tolya had set a trap. When the noise persisted, Olga opened the cellar door to see whether a rat had been caught. There on the stairs sat a being who resembled the satyrs and devils in medieval paintings. The creature was no bigger than two feet, and he sneered at Olga. With a rasping voice he said, 'I'll show you what I'm still able to do.'

Olga dropped the cellar door with a loud crash. She had always feared death and, like most Primorski people, believed in demons and house spirits. Yet, strangely, she wasn't that upset, and had a feeling that this evil spirit had been around for a long time already. Yet she shivered when she heard more tapping. She opened the window to let in the fresh spring air, and noticed a woodpecker hard at work. 'Thank heavens,' she thought, 'no more noise from the cellar.'

When Tolya returned that night, Olga related the strange event of that morning. Tolya reacted nervously. His conversion had been so recent. Quickly he summoned Yegor Betcher and Anatoli Khokha, his original new friends, and also his mother. After Olga repeated her story, they all knelt and prayed. Olga felt herself a hypocrite, kneeling but unable to pray. She would much rather have run away. Kneeling was the most humiliating thing a person could do, she felt. But as soon as the others began to pray, something strange happened. She felt herself become light as a feather, and lifted up above the ground. She had never felt this liberated, this clean, this rejuvenated and refreshed. All fear disappeared. That evening Olga even dared to go into the cellar by herself.

Now she became curious about faith and received daily instruction from Yegor and Anatoli. She changed visibly, even though her marriage had not completely recovered from all its previous wounds.

Viktor and Mariya Walter kept close contact with this recently converted couple, but their support had its limits. Tolya and Olga themselves had to decide to obey the Word of God before they could grow in faith. 'It's the same for every member of our congregation,' said Viktor, 'and that's the essence of our community: no words but deeds.'

But what about the baptism of the Holy Spirit?' asked Tolya who had already encountered that saying a few times. Viktor replied, 'It's all of a piece. I notice your longing for it. OK, do what the Bible tells you and pray for it. Then you will be baptized with the Holy Spirit.'

After this particular conversation with Viktor, Tolya came home late that evening. He tried not to wake anybody and he read a bit in the Bible. He had read the epistle of James before, but now it seemed that every word of it spoke to him directly. He felt himself greatly moved, and his heart overflowed with gratitude for God's love and redemption.

Then he heard Olga's voice from the bedroom. Tolya walked towards the door, but before he could open it he noticed she was praying, crying and laughing at the same time. 'No,' Tolya thought. 'I shouldn't disturb her.' He walked back and sank to his knees, only to feel clarity and light. He felt a tingling go through his whole body. It seemed that many shutters, doors and windows were being opened. With his hands held high he praised his heavenly Father and he heard himself speaking in tongues. While Tolya felt himself so close to God, his mind remained wonderfully calm and sober. He even crawled backwards a bit for fear of being burned by the stove. A previously unknown quiet and peace took over the whole house.

Then he thought about Olga. Very carefully he opened the bedroom door. There she sat, beaming. She too had been baptized by the Holy Spirit. For the first time in years they embraced each other. Tears streamed down their faces. Now they had the courage to pray together, and they weren't shy with each other any more. That night they confessed all the things that had kept them apart, to God and to each other. Only now, six years after the official ceremony, did they really feel married.

11
Counter Attack

In many respects 1981 had been a blessed year for the Chuguyevka congregation, what with the move, the new jobs, the splendid news that Central Asian congregations had continued to prosper even without the direct support of their sponsoring congregation, and the new mission posts that had been established in Primorski. The Chuguyevka congregation had overwhelming evidence that God Himself had led them to this mission field.

Each Sunday morning about a hundred and fifty people came to worship, including children who would sit in the first few rows, according to tradition.

God blessed them also with material things. Procuring food was not a simple matter for anybody in the Soviet Union. Large families especially spent a good deal of time supplementing the little that could be bought in stores. These Christians worked well together. Some were gifted in growing vegetables and potatoes, others in husbandry that produced meat and dairy products. Yegor Betcher and Samuel Walter were expert bee-keepers and both obtained permission to rent a piece of land in the forest for it. Together with old Christian Stumpf, who was a tinsmith, they built an impressive number of hives.

In late May, three months after Viktor had barely avoided arrest in Akhangaran, the 'Walter Case' files arrived at the Vladivostok KGB office, causing plenty of consternation. The KGB called the Tashkent office to inquire why the papers had taken such a long time. 'We have already given Walter permission to live here and build houses!' They quickly visited Chuguyevka and were displeased to discover how far advanced construction already was. They summoned Viktor to their offices that same day.

The head of the KGB in Chuguyevka, Lieutenant-Colonel Bykov, received him. With a look meant to impress, he showed Viktor the large Akhangaran file. 'I guess you know why we have called you', he said. Viktor looked him straight in the eye and nodded. He was wary. He had dealt with the KGB often enough to know that he was at the entrance of a trap, where each word might be turned against him.

However, to his astonishment Bykov seemed to have only one worry this time. He had heard that the whole of the pentecostal congregation of Nakhodka, the second largest Primorski harbour city, had approached the authorities for permission to emigrate, a request that had evoked strong bureaucratic anger all the way to Moscow. Bykov only asked, 'Mr Walter, you have permission to live here, but is it your real intent to emigrate too, like that group from Nakhodka?' It was an easy question to answer: 'No sir, not at all.'

The KGB officer looked satisfied for the moment and concluded the interview. 'If you want to avoid troubles here, remember, no proselytizing.' When Viktor left the office he had a feeling that life in Chuguyevka would not continue this peacefully.

Valeri Chupin, regional head of the Office of Religious Affairs, came from Vladivostok with the specific purpose of persuading the pentecostal congregation to register officially. 'Then you won't have any problems', he said genially to the leaders. 'Registration is no longer a problem. You retain your freedom and we leave you in peace.' Viktor interjected, 'We have had bad experiences with registration.

Please tell us what the law states. What are the rights and duties of a registered church?'

'No problem,' said Chupin royally, 'I'll arrange for city hall to prepare a set of documents for you to pick up. Read them at your leisure and I'll come back later to hear your decision.'

He left full of good will. That same day one of the brothers picked up two books containing the laws which governed religious affairs, one describing the rights and duties of a registered church and another containing directions to the KGB to curtail the life of the Church! This latter book was actually a secret document, and the civil servant shouldn't have provided it, for now the fat was in the fire.

These Christians were astonished to discover the duties of all authorities. Not only the KGB, but teachers, civil servants, selected politicians and employers were obliged to make the lives of Christians miserable!

They also read the first book, only to find out that it too contained regulations they could not square with their convictions about obedience to God and the Bible.

Chupin returned in a few days. 'And did you consult the law? Any questions?' he began, full of enthusiasm. After a moment of silence Viktor replied, 'Mr Chupin, I'm afraid we must disappoint you. We did pick up the two law books. About the administrative directions we can be brief', and he put the document on the table. 'It's clear that its real agenda is to get rid of all Christians. But even in the official act we find elements we cannot accept. Apparently we can't organize special youth services and meetings for women, and we can't have children in our services. But we are not only a worship community but a life-style community too. You prohibit the church from offering social assistance, even to its own members. All that is in conflict with out own constitution and with the Word of God.'

Chupin sat frozen to his chair. He snatched the secret document from the table and exclaimed, 'Who gave you this?'

'Your own people at city hall.'

'They shouldn't have done that!' Angrily he stormed outside.

Soon the congregation faced the consequences. A Sunday morning service was interrupted by the police who wrote down the names of all those present.

On 31st October 1981 a meeting was held in the Chuguyevka 'House of Culture', to which the citizens living in and around the community were invited. Chupin came all the way from Vladivostok to preside. In a 'sermon' he described the stubbornness of those newcomers from Central Asia, and the advantages of registration. But Viktor Walter patiently explained why they had to refuse registration. Chupin soon lost his patience and went on the attack. 'Non-registered Christians, and especially non-registered pentecostals, are our last enemy. If we beat them, we've done our job.'

Some of the people agreed with him. They had been primed with information about the 'criminal past' of these pentecostal Christians. Chupin angrily ended the meeting. 'If you don't register voluntarily, we'll hound you until you do.'

The first arrests took place on 15th November. Christian Stumpf led worship that morning and Yegor Betcher was in the middle of preaching his sermon when the attack took place. They both received a sentence of fifteen days in a dirty, overcrowded police cell. Two days later, Elvira Stumpf, Christian's twenty-year-old daughter, was arrested because she had recited a poem in the service. She spent ten days among women convicts.

One week later the faithful were better prepared. As soon as the police entered they began taking photographs. Oleg

Lobanov, the community's official photographer, had brought two cameras, one with a roll of film and the other empty. When the police reached over to confiscate his camera, he gave them the empty one, and the full one was quickly put in a safe place by another brother.

A few weeks later a brother took two officers aside and told them, 'You've come here to persecute us, but from now on you must wait until we finish worshipping. Please attend the whole service and then you can take us all to gaol. Come with me, we've reserved seats of honour for you.' Before they could reply, he walked to the front and motioned them to follow. Meekly they followed their guide and took their seats on the front pew, with the children. There they sat for the whole service, with mixed feelings, of course. When the congregation was ready to pray communally, the pastor said, 'For the benefit of our guests, when we pray we all kneel down.' One of the two immediately knelt down, but the other pulled at his sleeve and snarled, 'What's the matter with you?' Startled his friend stood up again, but remained standing in a reverent posture. The other followed his example, also feeling that one simply cannot remain seated at holy moments.

The newspapers published articles about the congregation in which the leaders were branded as fascists. Other obscene stories continued accusations of sexual misconduct. These so-called journalists even cited Samuel Walter's old car as proof of the irresponsible lifestyle of these 'sectarians'.

'Why do they call us fascists?' the Christians asked the KGB. 'Not one journalist has visited us to find out the truth.' The KGB agent shrugged his shoulders. 'Must have been a mistake. We can't control everything.'

Over the first six weeks of harassment the police handed out fines for 1500 roubles, the equivalent of ten monthly family incomes. On 23rd December Viktor Walter and

Christian Stumpf travelled to Vladivostok to lodge a complaint with Chupin, but to now avail. Early in 1982 they visited Major Dobish, the Chuguyevka police chief, who didn't even listen and said. 'The investigation has been slow thus far, but that'll change.'

Viktor sensed a disagreement between the KGB and other authorities about the method of tackling the Christians and he said, 'If you persist with these actions, I'll notify the authorities in Moscow.' That got him another ten days in a police cell.

The original plan to divide the Chuguyevka congregation in three was no longer deemed prudent. The elders decided to work for greater unity instead. All the members were enjoined never to compromise. 'The KGB shouldn't be able to drive a wedge between us.' They realized how serious the situation was and knew that the prophesied persecutions were at hand. They made emergency plans for when Viktor and the other leaders would be imprisoned. They made a complete list of all adult members, with authority always to be passed on to the next name on the list, so as to prevent divisions. The plan even provided that the women would continue the work of the congregation if all the men were arrested.

Right at the start God had warned them that they would encounter difficult times, and the prophecy had made them strong and courageous. They knew that God's plan ensured them victory in the end. Nobody gave any thought to giving in to the proposals of people such as Chupin. Worship services continued, just as their evangelism and widespread Bible teaching did. Using two wrecked cars that had been restored and four motorcycles, a number of evangelistic teams spread out each week.

After the 'House of Culture' meeting and the newspaper articles, public interest in them increased. Almost all of the neighbours thought the Christians were pleasant and helpful people, very different from ordinary folk, and were amazed to read of the many accusations, knowing from their own experience that they were false. The Christians were always willing to help each other and people outside their community too, and they never asked for payment. Well then, if you ever thought that Marx had some good ideas, these people put them into practice!

Yet the people from the community never proselytized their particular lifestyle. Just as in Central Asia, they refrained from pushing their ideas of living together like the early Christians did. Curious people were always welcome to join for a time. Some did and stayed, although most of them found it impossible to change their own lives that much.

But joining wasn't necessary for everybody, as the Chuguyevka pentecostals often said. 'Living as we do is not the only way of being a Christian. God is much larger than the lives we are able to show.' The core of their mission work was the laying of biblical foundations in the lives of people. They preached the need for breaking with sin and the world, and living holy lives on the basis of the redemptive work of Jesus Christ, to the glory of God. Furthermore, their own lives exemplified freedom, as they no longer feared the people who opposed the Kingdom of God.

Nikolai Vins said: 'If you proclaim the Gospel and establish a congregation, you must be able to say, 'Come, have a look at how Christians live.' That's the most powerful recommendation. Our first goal is to strengthen solitary Christians and help them be a good example in their own environment. First be a light yourself, and then help others to be a light, and after that still others will be attracted to turn towards God also.'

The Chuguyevka evangelists were eminently practical. If they met a Christian who had lived alone for years and complained about loneliness, they would ask, 'Does anybody at work know you are a Christian?' Often the person would say no, and then they would offer this advice: 'OK, start by telling your colleagues at work that God loves them.' More often than not a fellow worker would also be present on their next visit.

No wonder that this congregation called forth the hatred of atheists who thought they had long ago rid Primorski of religion. They now realized that religious faith had launched a counter attack.

12
Who Really Owns Our Children?

It was clear that the KGB had begun a hate campaign. Even though many Chuguyevka citizens weren't ready to believe slanderous journalists, there were many who no longer knew how to be critical, or who had ulterior motives.

One evening Yevgeniya Lobsov came rushing into Viktor Walter's home. Before she even reached the living room she called out, 'Viktor! Viktor! Valeri is being beaten up. They're killing him!' Panting she stood in the door. Viktor had been talking to Tolya, and together they ran outside. They heard the shouting of drunken men. Three or four of them were hitting Valeri's motorcycle with iron bars. Valeri himself was nowhere to be seen. Perhaps he'd run away, for one of the fellows wore his jacket. The moment the men saw Tolya and Viktor the men too ran away, but from a distance yelled, 'Fascists, you are fascists. We'll show you what we'll do with you.'

Viktor and Tolya knew that these men lived a few houses down the street, and all had criminal records as a result of their thieving and violence. (One day they were to tell Viktor that in return for working for the KGB, their sentences would be suspended, and their prime job was harassing the new pentecostal congregation.)

When Viktor, Tolya and Valeri (who had re-emerged) reported the incident to the police and sought to lodge a complaint about the assault and destruction of a motorcycle, they were told to arrest the accused themselves and bring them to the police station. The brothers took a car and

found the drunken men in a short time. They managed to
bring in two of them and the police perfunctorily locked
them up for the night. The next morning one of them
pointed a gun at Viktor's home and said, 'I can do what
I want, the police will always let me go. If I were you, I'd
watch it, for I hate fascists.' He had probably read the
completely false tale in *The Red Banner* about an 'uncle'
of Viktor Walter who was supposed to have been
commandant of a German concentration camp for
Russians. He was accused of having personally executed
a large number of his prisoners.

The Chuguyevka Christians were determined to leave
their defence to God, but they realised the danger of giving
in to fear. Both adults and children were constantly in
prayer, asking God to protect their hearts from the
influences of fear and doubt. Nobody used the streets
without urgent need. Even when they were together on
their way back from services, the road wasn't always safe.
Often gangs of drunken fellows armed with clubs were
waiting to beat them up.

Not only the streets, but their own homes became unsafe.
When Wilhelm Rosher came home one evening from a
church council meeting, he discovered that his front porch
had been burned black. With tears on her face his wife Anna
stood looking at the devastation. The same bandits who had
attacked Valeri Lobsov had thrown a gasoline bomb inside.
She had gone to bed early and hadn't noticed, but passers-
by had seen the sudden flames at the front door and had
immediately taken action. By the time Anna and the
children were awake, most of the danger had passed.

Next, a heavy brick was thrown through Viktor Walter's
window into the children's bedroom while they were
sleeping, and with such force that even the wooden window
frame had been splintered. It was a miracle that the children
hadn't been badly hurt. From that point on no one let his

children sleep behind windows; they could only sleep behind a wall.

The KGB were busy brooding about a final solution, and in 1982 tried many ways to harass the Chuguyevka Christians. For instance, a senior officer who had the responsibility of calling up military recruits, discovered that all the men in the congregation had refused to bear arms. This major, and his right hand captain Anykin, loathed all Christians, pentecostal ones in particular. The two officers decided to call up all the men for reservist training. Even Viktor Walter, who had the word 'invalid' on his military pass, had to serve for two months. Anykin made a special visit to Viktor to tell him that he personally would guarantee the pastor a miserable time. When Viktor reported to the army base, they demanded that he swear the military oath. Smiling, Viktor said, 'I didn't do it then, and you don't really think that I'll do it now, do you, being the father of a large family?'

If enmity had been directed to adults only, the troubles would have been bearable, but when the children were made targets, it became impossible not to react.

The attitude of school teachers was especially hard to fathom. How could the minds of pedagogues be so twisted? How could they lose their humanity in the name of 'scientific atheism'?

The new students didn't participate in the political curriculum and resolutely refused to join the communist youth movement. The girls continued to wear kerchiefs on their heads, even during physical education. Their behaviour caused lots of teacher talk. The school staff called for help from a specialist at the school board, who had close contact with the KGB. The net tightened.

Now and then some of the teachers attended a worship service to see whether their children were present, contrary to the law. They would demonstratively look around and listen critically to songs and preaching. They knew in advance that it was bad for a child's mental health to be in church, especially a pentecostal church.

But they were astonished to notice how eagerly the children sang the hymns, and how free and joyous they were in the company of other Christians. Most remarkable of all, the children participated freely in the congregational prayer.

Did the teacher hear aright? Did her student pray for her? Sure, it was true! She spotted a seven-year-old from her classroom praying for his teacher, his eyes closed so tight and his face so serious! What made him think that she had any sympathy for this sectarian business? Admittedly, the hymns were nice, and she herself had even tapped her feet a bit, but surely this little one wouldn't think that his teacher would have faith in fairy tales?

She looked around during the prayer. Everyone sat with eyes closed. To her surprise she spotted Anya from a higher grade, whom she knew not to belong here. 'What is she doing here? She's a member of the *komsomol* (the communist youth movement)', the teacher thought, almost aloud.

She knew what she had to do. This religious virus should not be allowed to gain ground. Anya would serve as a deterrent.

The next day a special meeting was called for all students who were members of the *komsomol*. The principal of the school spoke: 'In Chuguyevka things are happening which we as a communist youth movement must oppose. Anya was present at a pentecostal worship service yesterday, and we know it wasn't her first time. She'll have to choose. If she goes once more she can't remain a member. Of course she'll lose all her special youth privileges. I hope you'll understand that the same will happen to anyone who attends these sectarian meetings, even out of mere curiosity.' After that public humiliation Anya never showed up in church again.

The school was utterly devoted to its task as defender of atheist thinking, abandoning all humanity in its zeal. Violence, deceit, threats and harassment were permitted. The ends justified the means.

It was as if time had stood still in Primorski. Twenty years after their parents had been accused of being Nazis, the same abuse was heaped upon the children. As part of the curriculum, old war movies were shown, with the result that hatred against children of German descent waxed once more. Every break, every walk to and from school, and every encounter with other children grew to be a heavy burden. Teachers would simply turn away from beatings and kicking. Increasingly, the children would come home crying and upset.

Some parents were at their wit's end. Conversations with teachers and the principal were impossible, for there was little difference between them and the KGB, or so it seemed. If a mother lamented that her daughter was afraid to go to school, she was accused of being a religious fanatic. The teacher would say, 'It's your own fault. Why does your child have to be different from the others? You are twisting your child's mind with your ideas about God and heaven.'

After a church service attended by the KGB and the superintendent of education, five sets of parents were summoned. Romanov, the superintendent, said, 'If you let 'our' children attend services from now on, we shall take steps to bring them up ourselves. You don't seem to realize that all Soviet children are the property of the state, and we have the duty to raise them in the spirit of Lenin and in the doctrines of scientific atheism. We have received permission from Moscow to take away your children if you persist in tormenting them spiritually.'

The parents reacted with great indignation. Vladimir

Walter said, 'God is the Creator of all that lives. Our children are His first of all. We as parents have the duty to raise them into human beings who obey God. We shall never obey the authorities before God. Moreover, it's my wife who has borne these children and you haven't had to exert any effort.'

Four parents received a fine of eighty roubles, and Viktor Walter one of 'only' thirty, because his daughter was in the early grades. In total, the Chuguyevka congregation was fined six thousand roubles in eighteen months. Anatoli Khokha earned a monthly salary of 160 roubles for his family of nine children, and he stated that he would have to find a second job to pay his many fines. Angrily Romanov said: 'We'll see to it that you won't find another job anywhere.' Nevertheless, the conversation ended with this clear parental answer: 'We'll never give up our children!'

But this January 1983 confrontation proved to be a turning point. A West German relative of Nikolai Vins had invited him to visit. Nikolai had almost forgotten the letter, for why go to Germany? He belonged in Chuguyevka, and as much as anyone he was convinced of the need to proclaim the Gospel there. But the threats from the authorities reminded him of the letter. They all knew that an emigration application was an effective way to scare the KGB. Emigration requests had to go through Moscow and would result in international publicity in the West. Perhaps it was the only way to force the KGB to stop harassing them. The Russian secret service normally operates behind the scenes, employing henchmen for the dirty work and trying to remain invisible.

The proposal to accept the invitation by Nikolai Vins's relative was discussed by the church council. It took a number of meetings to make the point of it clear to everyone. Their desire to emigrate was not prompted by a wish for a higher standard of living, but only a response to the attack on their parenthood and a defence of their children's right of choice. They wrote an extensive and detailed account of all the past threats, fines and incarcerations that ended with: 'Parenthood is a blessing and a right God gives to people. No government may appropriate this right.'

They sent the letter, together with the passports of all members of the congregation and emigration applications, to the Moscow authorities, on 30th March 1983.

A few days later Viktor Walter was summoned to the local police station. He was told that he would be tried and was taken to the office of the public prosecutor. The man obviously hadn't heard about the letter to Moscow, for he asked for Viktor's papers. 'Those are in Moscow', Viktor said, and explained that all of his friends' passports had been sent to the highest authorities in Moscow. The public prosecutor realized that he could no longer act on his own and that he would have to justify himself to the Supreme Soviet in Moscow. For the moment, Viktor could return home.

At first the decision to apply for emigration seemed to have positive effects. A certain Tarasov came all the way from Moscow to mediate between the Chuguyevka Christians and the regional government. In the presence of a high local functionary he asked whether 'the unjustified part of the fines' had been returned yet. Amazed, Viktor looked at the man and said, 'I didn't even know you had decided that. For my part, the whole of the fines were unjustified, but we haven't seen a cent.'

The Chuguyevka civil servant brazenly lied that he had repaid everything. Viktor told the Moscow man: 'Mr Tarasov, if he lies that much when you're here, think how much he lies when you're back in Moscow!' The fines were never repaid, but the bureaucrat was sacked shortly afterwards.

Life for the congregation became increasingly difficult. Children in school, as well as parents at work, were harassed. Whole work forces were called together to be warned against the pentecostal threat. Of course many fellow workers didn't believe the stories of ritual killings of children, sex orgies and spiritual tyranny. They had experienced these Christians to be reliable, kind and hard working people. But when the KGB put on the pressure, many were prepared to violate their conscience and sacrifice truth for security.

Dark clouds began to overshadow the happy initial months in Chuguyevka. Yet no one panicked. The Akhangaran experience had been an excellent training, for there they had learned to share both joy and sorrow. The certainty that God had prophesied this road of suffering and resistance was an enormous consolation. God knew their worries and problems, and He would bring deliverance. Even in this situation there were still plenty of things to enjoy together.

At home the children learned quickly to forget their school experiences. Mum and Dad taught them not to hate in return, and parents frequently visited the principal to protest. They explained to the children why it was difficult to be a Christian in the Soviet Union. Early in their lives children learned that they had to make choices. Through trial and error they learned to be children of God, trusting His protection even as they walked through coals of fire.

13
A Wild Chase

Chuguyevka, 1983

Sunday became a very busy day for the police and the KGB. At first it was easy to discover where the church services took place, but the congregation got tired of having their services disrupted. Seeing the most important moments of congregational life rudely terminated was intolerable. Those services were an essential component of the growth of spiritual life, more important even than daily food. So they decided to trick the KGB.

They began to vary both meeting days and times. That necessitated having to use some Sundays to catch up with essential work. For example, one Sunday in February 1983 was used to remove a large quantity of previously cut fire wood from the forest. Vladimir Walter obtained his employer's permission to use the crane lorry he chauffeured at work. Early in the morning he and his helpers took off.

The KGB had just recruited local police, some *komsomol* young people and the 'Druzhiniki', the auxiliary constabulary, to help them discover where the services would be held that day. A guard was posted in front of each pentecostal house at 7:00 a.m. Any householder who left was followed, including Vladimir and his friends. Shortly after they arrived at the forest they were surrounded by police, who asked Vladimir, 'Who gave you permission to use a state-owned crane for private business?' Vladimir mentioned his foreman's name, but the police accused him of theft and took his driver's licence.

The next day Vladimir had to give an account of his

actions, and to his consternation his boss denied having given him permission to use the lorry. His licence was confiscated, and he couldn't work as crane operator any more. Luckily many colleagues protested against this unjust action and after a week Vladimir got his licence back.

Some Christians asked Dobish, the local police chief, when all this harassment would stop. All he said was, 'We're soldiers. We only follow orders. When the orders stop we shall stop.'

The threat of Christians losing their jobs gradually increased. Thousands of roubles were steadily deducted from their pay, resulting in great financial hardship for the community. One way or another they had to find additional sources of income. Yet it was also remarkably obvious how God showed His power more as persecutions increased. Very early they had been able to buy some cows, and so babies and expectant mothers always received enough milk. Meat was also in good supply, for they owned their own modest pig farm. For the moment they had enough food.

The neighbours were amazed at the Christians. A rumour floated around that they even knew in advance when it would rain. These newcomers to the district were always right on time getting hay inside, even if their neighbour's hay was rotting in the field. A few times the whole area was drenched in heavy rains, while on the hay fields of the Christians the sun kept shining. One neighbour decided to watch his Christian neighbours closely and follow them in their work patterns, a decision he never regretted.

Regularly the community received help. For instance, somehow spotted a swarm of bees surrounding a queen high up in a tree and told Yegor Betcher, 'If you can catch them, you can have them.' Yegor got stung dozens of times, but he managed to capture the swarm. After some time the community owned more than fifty hives in the forest clearing, about twelve miles away, and the yearly yield amounted to an enormous two thousand litres of honey.

That small clearing in the midst of a dense forest became an important gathering place for forest products. The men built a small cabin for overnight stays and for storing tools. It was also an excellent shelter for forest workers, who would stay in the forest for many days during the summer. The taiga was a rich source of products the city would pay good prices for: edible mushrooms, berries, wild grapes and medicinal roots from plants in the ginseng family. Pulling those widespread and tough roots was a heavy job, requiring men to wear a broad leather belt, around which they wound an iron chain, with a sturdy hook at the end. First they bared a portion of the root with a shovel, and then they attached the hook and pulled with all their strength.

Members of the community loved the outdoors and in summer they often went together to mow wild grass in remote fields as fodder for the cattle, for they were not permitted to own their own land. They got permission to gather their fodder that way, even though an occasional hostile and vengeful person drove his own cattle over those just-mown fields, solely to harass them. But the Christians didn't let themselves to intimidated or robbed of their joy. Their communal bonds increased constantly under the pressure of the difficulties.

They joyfully sang while they worked. In their spare time they swam in the Ussuri river or picnicked in a field or forest. Wherever they were, they also used time to pray together. Having talks with God simply belonged to their daily routine, and wasn't meant to be a form of ritualized piety.

Not much time was spent on conversations regarding complicated spiritual topics, for everyone was too busy with practical matters. However, enough time was always reserved for prayer.

Gradually the congregation settled on fixed prayer times. The first prayer would take place within the family at 6:00 in the morning, then at 10:00 a.m. and 1:00 p.m. members would pray wherever they found themselves, and finally at 7:00 in the evening family prayers would be held again. Those steady prayer times never became a fixed law, but that Soviet school of hard religious knocks had demonstrated the wisdom of developing beneficial traditions and habits while having the opportunity to do so. They said to themselves, 'If persecution should come, you may not have time to think about how to stand firm. All you will have to fall back on is habits of endurance and faithfulness.'

Monitoring all the activities of the Chuguyevka Christians became a mammoth task for the small army of KGB agents, police officers, city hall bureaucrats and detectives, and sometimes comic situations developed.

Christian and Nelie Stumpf were guarding the beehives one day when suddenly chief detective Tulnov confronted them. He knew they had gathered medicinal roots the day before and he wanted to harass his arch-enemies. Seeing the large pile of roots, he commanded Christian to load them into his car. The old man refused and called his wife. Tulnov was a large and powerful man, and he probably felt foolish bickering about some roots in the presence of a woman, so he changed tactics. 'Do you have a rifle?' he asked, walking towards the cabin as if to inspect it. He knew that both Yegor Betcher and Tolya Sheludkov owned guns and had applied for a hunting permit, which had been refused on the grounds that 'Christians cannot be trusted with weapons'. Christian in turn knew that Tulnov often poached animals himself and replied, 'Comrade Tulnov, when we see a rabbit, we call it and put some salt on its tail so that we can pick it up with our hands. Don't tell me you're accusing us of something we could accuse you of? Close by in the forest I found a red deer skin. You wouldn't know anything about that, would you? Why do you come here to bore us with stories about roots which we gathered with a lot of effort?'

Right then Christian heard the sound of Yegor Betcher's motorcycle. Tulnov knew he couldn't score this time and he went off.

After a long day of work Viktor Walter stood washing himself in a creek close to the cabin. Yegor and Tolya walked into the forest with their dog Barsik, a white Laika, a breed only known in the Soviet Union. Barsik was well trained and Yegor would know from her barking and growling whether danger loomed or game was around. When the two men were about a hundred and twenty yards into the forest, the dog growled. This is how Yegor later told the story.

'I knew that Barsik had smelt game and I told Tolya to load his gun. He laughed and said, 'You take that dog far too seriously'. But when I put two bullets in my own gun, he followed suit. Then I let the dog go. We hadn't heard anything, but Barsik knew where to go, and as if shot from a bow she disappeared into the forest. No more than a few seconds later we heard the dog's wild growling and hysterical barking. We ran towards the sound, but stopped dead in our tracks after no more than thirty yards, for there stood an enormous black bear, as tall as a fully grown man. The animal wildly batted his paws in the air and came towards us. Barsik hung on his back and sunk her teeth into the bear's neck. The dog wouldn't let go, tearing her head wildly to and fro. I knew that a black bear is much more dangerous than his brown cousin, and I also knew that Barsik wouldn't let go voluntarily, so an accurate shot was our only chance. The colossal animal sank to its knees, still alive. Barsik was still holding on and I didn't dare shoot any higher for fear of hitting the dog. Carefully I approached the bear with my long hunting knife. The animal appeared to be dying, but when I lifted my knife he raised himself again. 'Shoot, Tolya', I said, and at the same moment Tolya's bullet hit the animal in the head. Only then did Barsik let go.

'I loved that dog, and I was sad that Barsik was eaten by a tiger not long after. Primorski still counts a number of Siberian tigers. One night I stood eye to eye with this cunning, yet gorgeous animal. I heard Barsik wildly pulling on her chain and carelessly I walked towards her to see what was the matter. I saw that she had crawled into the dog house, which was unusual as she normally slept outside. Walking back to the cabin my flashlight shone into the forest and there, no more than twenty feet away, stood an enormous tiger. He had meant to capture the dog, but I wouldn't be the first human to be victim of this bandit. As loudly as I could I roared, 'Go away, off with you!' The animal stood still, softly growling while baring his teeth. Only the end of his tail swept from left to right. To this day I don't know how I did it, but with one jump I got into the cabin, grabbed whatever lids and chains I could and made as enormous a racket as I could manage. With a few elegant jumps the predator disappeared into the forest. He didn't return that night, but now he knew where he could find prey. A few weeks later I came too late, for he had taken the dog, chain and all.'

Confronting predators was child's play compared to confronting the ever present KGB. The number of agents increased daily.

The brothers had decided not to be stopped from their main objective of preaching the Gospel. Much to the chagrin of the KGB they managed to circumvent road barriers and inspection posts, and continued their work. By day or night the small congregations were visited every week, and the brothers made many trips to solitary

Christians who craved contact with fellow believers. God was always near and did not permit them to be trapped, even though some of the escapes were in the nick of time.

Once Viktor Walter and four young people travelled to the pentecostal church of Nakhodka. This city has an important naval base which can easily be cut off from the rest of the district. Checkpoints with barriers and barbed wire fences are placed everywhere around the whole city.

The Chuguyevka evangelistic team was in double jeopardy here, for it had neither passports nor identity cards, since both of these had been sent to Moscow. But even these missing travel documents could not hold them back from their purpose.

Viktor Walter came this time because the congregation needed to celebrate communion. The young people formed a small chorus. The large Nakhodka pentecostal congregation had split in two over a dispute about registration, and the Chuguyevka people tried to minister to the un-registered part of it. Viktor knew that the KGB was busy infiltrating this segment, and that he could expect traitors among them, but that was no reason to abandon these poor people, even though other pastors had done so.

The service was marvellous, most certainly worth the long trip over snow-covered, narrow mountain roads, worth also the risk of traitors who undoubtedly would receive Judas wages in exchange for information.

Soon after the group had started the return trip, Viktor spotted a suspicious car following them. Twice he suddenly took a side street, but the car stayed behind them. He drove as fast as he could, but the pursuer got right on the tail of Viktor's old Volga. Soon they were overtaken and forced to stop. Plain-clothes men blocked all four doors. Viktor rolled down his window and and looked straight into the unmistakable face of a KGB agent. 'Step outside', the man said. 'What do you want from me?' Viktor asked. 'Step outside, I want to see your papers.' Viktor realized that they wanted to arrest him far from home, already knowing he didn't have papers. He motioned as if to open the car door and the man stepped back, but Viktor stamped on the accelerator, and before they could stop him, they were in full flight, through inhospitable country where no one would find them for days in the event of an accident. Viktor and his young friends prayed as loudly as they could, 'God send us your angels and bring us safely home!'

It didn't take the KGB car long to catch up, but one way or another Viktor stayed ahead of them. The road grew more narrow and the sky ever darker. Sometimes the two headlights only showed a deep precipice. For two long hours they drove through the taiga at breakneck speed, two frightening hours in which they escaped death several times. Finally they arrived at a residential area and the KGB agents slunk away like hyenas, for they weren't willing to be recognized. Their plan to arrest the pentecostal leader far from the protection of other believers had failed.

The next day the Chuguyevka KGB paid Viktor a visit. The man pretended to be jovial. 'Boy, boy, you're a fast driver. My colleagues had a brand new car but they could barely keep up with your old Volga.' And with a generous gesture he added, 'All right, we forgive you. You'll get away with ten days in jail for breaking traffic laws.'

The Christians had agreed to immediately visit anyone who received a visit by the KGB. As soon as a stranger entered any garden gate, all the children ran out to warn the others. This way all heard the KGB agreements and proposals, and the KGB could not sow dissent amongst them.

The same happened today, and soon the man was surrounded by other members of the congregation. Now that Viktor was out of the deserted taiga he didn't mind going to the police station. The KGB couldn't do much, for he would keep absolutely quiet during interrogations. In Nakhodka the KGB had been successful in sowing dissent, but they would fail in Chuguyevka.

The congregation had willingly accepted the commission to preach the Gospel to sinners, but it objected to preaching to KGB members, whom they considered as henchmen of the devil. Perhaps we Westerners would think such a stance intolerant, but without it the pentecostal church of Chuguyevka could not have maintained unity. Dozens of congregations in the Soviet Union had become KGB victims when individual Christians, often elders and deacons, engaged agents in conversation. Often without knowing it themselves, they were then used to sow dissent or force registration.

The Chuguyevka congregation was the subject of discussion amongst atheists, but also among pentecostals throughout the Soviet Union, especially about their communal lifestyle. Critique was not unusual and people who judge quickly will always believe the wildest stories. Other pentecostals heard all kinds of things, without taking the trouble to find out that the origins of many stories resided in the imagination of so-called journalists, who in truth were KGB agents. Some leaders of other congregations even demanded that the Chuguyevka congregation be expelled from 'the Brotherhood of Pentecostals' on the basis of these rumours. Happily, not everyone was in favour of such an unspiritual approach.

Bishop Sergei Sakharovich arrived in Chuguyevka on 1st January 1984, having travelled many thousands of miles. This elderly man shepherded the pentecostal church of Kishinev in the Soviet Republic of Moldavia. Primorski was forbidden territory for him and he travelled in the greatest of secrecy. He too had heard about the problems here between pentecostals and the authorities, the wild tales of sexual misconduct, child abuse and theft of state property. But he was a genuine spiritual leader and did not judge on the basis of rumours. He had come to Chuguyevka to see for himself and hear the truth of the stories.

The brothers were delighted with his visit. After long conversations he embraced the elders and blessed them in their difficult work. Bishop Sergei counselled: 'Stand fast in your faith, for your witness will mean a turning point for all pentecostal congregations. If you lose heart, general persecution will return. Be of good courage and persevere in this righteous struggle.'

This encouragement came at an important moment, for the most difficult time was just about to begin.

14
A Mysterious Death

By July 1983 it had already been four months since they had sent their passports to Moscow. An official whose task it was to authorize travel documents came from Vladivostok to Chuguyevka. Colonel Spirin invited fifty members of the congregation to discuss their request to leave the Soviet Union. But when they appeared at city hall, the man proved to be an old Stalinist, full of prejudice against Germans.

'You'll have to take your passports back', he said threateningly. He had no kindness in him, for he added, 'There's not a chance that we'll let you leave the Soviet Union. I have fought fascism for five years and you are of the same ilk. The only way you'll leave this country is via a rope around your neck.'

Calmly they explained to him that it was the legal right of all Soviet citizens to travel to wherever they wanted and know they were welcome. 'Those laws were not meant for your kind. You have no rights at all!' he barked.

When they refused to take back their passports, he gave orders to the city hall clerks to refuse registration of births, marriages and deaths. When in those days three children were born and their names could not be registered, the Chuguyevka church began to maintain its own register, witnessing each record with two signatures.

Their request for emigration was refused. The Supreme Soviet had become acquainted with their situation, but it hadn't helped them. Now what should they do?

Emigration had not been their principal objective. Their

applications were meant to be the means by which they could expose the illegal acts of local authorities. Routine appeals were useless.

'Now we need special wisdom from God', observed Viktor Walter. 'The Word of God says: "If someone is in need of wisdom, then let him pray for it to God, who will give it, simply and without reproach." Therefore we must pray, pray more than we now do. I also propose that those who can, participate in a fast.' His proposal was immediately accepted, for only a direct intervention by God could change so troubled a situation.

Seventy Christians in all refrained from eating. Those who fasted more than a day stayed away from their jobs, as they did not know what effect the fast would have on their ability to work. Twenty children between the ages of seven and eleven voluntarily didn't touch their food for twenty-four hours. Sixteen women who were pregnant or breast-feeding little babies participated for three days. Eleven other women fasted five days, and the remaining twenty-three men, ten days.

They spent much time in prayer, and experienced God providing them with strength. The first three days were the most difficult. After that they felt much better. They also gained clarity about what God wanted them to do. Everyone grew more convinced than ever that they couldn't give up. The future of their children, and of the Church of Jesus Christ in the Soviet Union, was at stake. Bishop Sergei had said it: they had to remain steadfast and not retreat one step. Together they decided to continue to travel this road.

After more threats directed against them, they wrote another letter to the authorities to announce another fast if they didn't get permission to emigrate. They also wrote to the governments in Moscow and West Germany, as well as to the United Nations. In all their letters they announced that they would begin an official hunger strike on 12th January 1984.

On 23rd December 1983, Viktor Walter and twenty brothers were invited to appear at city hall for talks. KGB Lieutenant-Colonel Bykov and one Shevchenko from the provincial authorities told them that almost everything had been arranged. Four families could leave in March, and if the others could show West German entry visas, their road would be clear too. Of course, they had to promise not to begin their hunger strike. 'Try us,' Shevchenko said, 'if we don't keep our word you can always send your passports away again and begin your hunger strike.'

It sounded promising, almost too good to be true. The twenty-one men took their passports back and completed the applications for exit visas. Four months later they were notified that all applications had been denied 'for criminal reasons'. Even the official who told them didn't know what that meant.

The Chuguyevka Christians knew what they had to do. They sent their passports to Moscow again and announced the start of their hunger strike on 15th September 1984. Participation was limited to adult volunteers. Children, expectant mothers and mothers of small babies were not included, for this fast would be more than just a few days.

The men took unpaid leave of absence. They did not know what the consequences would be, but the situation was urgent enough. School had become impossible for the children. More and more often these 'nazi children' became targets of harassment. Of course conditions at work also deteriorated steadily. The fasters openly told their employers the reasons for their action. Their fellow workers showed plenty of sympathy, and considered the actions of the authorities excessive. Their own children had also told them how Christian children were targets of beatings and prejudicial treatment. They knew that these people were not criminals. Most of the men didn't smoke or drink, and they always worked hard to provide for their often large families. By contrast, many enterprises in the area produced only at half-speed after the workers had been paid, for almost every worker drank to excess and then didn't report for work.

However, in Primorski the KGB decided who was a valuable worker and who wasn't. Foremen were put under pressure to make the lives of Christian workers difficult, and, if they refused, they were in danger of losing their own jobs.

The announcement of the hunger strike provided the anonymous KGB journalist with a reason to write new copy. Obviously, the pentecostals were bent on publicity and had invented something new. 'They have begun a hunger strike. However, the architect of it, Samuel Walter, an elderly man sixty years old, has taken his leave. He pretends to have the flu and has a princely room in the Vladivostok hospital, where he is spoiled by attractive nurses, while his so-called brothers and sisters are starving. Actually, don't take that too seriously either, for the carefully kept secret of these sectarians has been discovered. During the day they pretend not to eat, but at night the blinds are carefully closed and they have a merry time of gorging themselves at a groaning table.'

Who to believe, that newspaper or those Christians who on principle even refrained from defending themselves? Their fasting was a cry to God for help. But they knew they were being watched, and therefore they attached painted signs to their houses with the Russian word GOLODOVKA, or hunger strike. Underneath this was written: 'This is the second last time we fast. Let us emigrate in accordance with the constitution of the Soviet Union.'

Moreover, they invited an independent medical team to

certify that they weren't taking any food, two doctors from Vladivostok and one from Chuguyevka, together with government witnesses. Happily, the doctors were no KGB instruments. They examined all the participants, and advised some of the weaker ones to drink more fluids. Those doctors became convinced that this group of people were in dire spiritual need, and their fasting was born of utter despair.

Of course, KGB honour was now at stake, for these Christians hadn't yielded one inch and had managed to defy the mightiest institution in the Soviet Union. That kind of thing had not happened before and the defiance had to be crushed. The KGB looked for every opportunity to destroy these 'pentecostal sectarians', and even resorted to murder.

Samuel Walter may have been sixty years old, but he was as healthy and strong as ever. Every summer's day he went to the forest cabin to look after the bees, and even lent a hand in the forest on occasion. He had caught a cold in late August, after he got wet and spent a night in the drafty cabin. The next day he complained about pains in his loins and was feverish. The doctor told him, 'You should go to the hospital, that'll cure you quickly.'

They brought him to the Vladivostok hospital, which had a good reputation. Moreover, one of Samuel's cousins worked in it. The fever didn't let up and the examination took a long time, so he stayed there for a few weeks. Samuel was sad that he could not participate in the fasting. His wife Frida returned before the middle of September to take part in the prayers and fasting. Of course she visited him regularly, as did his other relatives. Moreover, Vladimir Popatov, Samuel's cousin, kept an eye on him too.

When rumours about the hunger strike reached Vladivostok, the hospital atmosphere was negatively affected. The specific accusation against Samuel also made the rounds. One October day when Frida was waiting in the hallway for a doctor to finish his work with her husband, she heard the doctor address him in a rough way. An uncomfortable feeling came over her. 'Why do they treat him badly?' she thought.

As the doctor was leaving, he sneered, 'We'll fix you up soon, Samuel.' He looked surprised when he saw Frida in the hall and told her, 'You can take him home again next week. You'd better bring some clothes.' All day Frida stayed with her husband and she noticed that he was improving. She told him the stories that were making the rounds in Primorski. Samuel listened and told his wife that he had noticed a high KGB officer talking to the chief physician. He worried and wondered if he should be collected sooner.

When Frida returned home, plans to collect Samuel were made immediately. When a KGB agent asked them the next day whether they owned a grave in case Samuel should die, they knew they couldn't wait any longer.

Viktor was away in Moscow, where in great secrecy he was informing foreign diplomats of the situation. Hence it was Vladimir who decided to take Nikolai and his mother along to pick up his Dad from Vladivostok.

That evening (14th October 1984), the last day of the hunger strike, a telegram arrived for Frida Walter. At first they thought it had come from Moscow, but instead the hospital had sent it: 'Come immediately to Vladivostok. Your husband is in critical condition.' Within an hour they were on their way.

Early the next morning they arrived. Samuel had been moved to the eighth floor. 'Why there? He's always been on the fourth', Frida asked. Vladimir supported his mother who had grown weak because of the fasting. They had to climb the stairs, because the lift was out of order. When they arrived upstairs, they heard that Samuel had already died the previous evening, even before the telegram had been sent.

Frida was crushed. In despair, she sat at her husband's bedside, still clutching the bag with his clean clothes. She had so counted on taking him home, in spite of the telegram.

But something was amiss. That KGB question about the grave . . .' The strange behaviour of the doctor. Moreover, several people had been refused access to Samuel during that last week. Vladimir asked for the cause of death. The physician told him it was a circulation problem, an embolism or something. However, intern cousin Vladimir Popatov told them that he had visited Samuel the afternoon before. He had been deathly ill and could only point to his mouth to indicate he was thirsty. He had given him some water, which Samuel couldn't even drink any more, and he had fought death from two in the afternoon until 9.30 in the evening.

'Then it wasn't an embolism', Vladimir posed. 'Perhaps not', his cousin answered. Frida demanded an autopsy. Now suddenly the authorities told her that lung cancer had been the cause of death. What cruelty and insensitivity! One lie after another.

'No', said the young cousin, who wanted to become a doctor and who was naïve to boot. 'That can't be true. Doctors don't lie.' He didn't even doubt his colleague when he told Popatov, 'I didn't know you were related to this man. You should have told me. Didn't you know he was a dangerous enemy of the state?'

Frida, Vladimir and Nikolai remained in Vladivostok for those terrible days. The doctors first told them that they would only release the body after they saw proof of ownership of a grave in Vladivostok. Vladimir went out to purchase a grave, but when he returned he noticed great unease, and nobody, not even Frida, was allowed near the body. When Vladimir showed his proof of purchase, a doctor said, 'Who told you that you had to do that? You can take him to Chuguyevka, but only in an enclosed lorry.' The next day, already Wednesday, they were finally able to borrow a lorry from a Vladivostok brother. When they arrived at the hospital a very different mood met them. 'Why did you borrow a lorry?' the doctor asked kindly. 'You could have taken him in your own car.'

When they put the dead man in a casket, they noticed that the whole length of his chest had been cut open, and the rough stitches told them that the operation had taken place after Samuel's death. Nikolai said, 'That's why they sent us from pillar to post. They had to remove the evidence of the real cause of death.' No one answered him, but the three Chuguyevka Christians knew. They carefully carried the casket down and laid it on the floor of the old Volga. Silently they drove the long way home.

Viktor had returned from Moscow in the meantime. He had brought some fresh fruit, telling Mayiya: 'Look, I bought them especially for Dad. It'll make him better soon.' His wife said, 'Viktor, your father is no longer alive. He died Sunday evening.'

Viktor was shocked. He didn't move from his chair as he heard the story of the sudden and mysterious death of his father. All kinds of thoughts flitted through his brain. 'Lord, we fasted and prayed for one whole month. Is this your answer?' God reminded him of the words he had already heard nine years ago. 'I shall lead your feet through fire and test your lifestyle. Your pastor shall be imprisoned.' That was it! Samuel had always been the oldest, and the pastor in the eyes of the KGB. It was Samuel they summoned when they felt like it. Now his dear father was dead. He could no longer intercept the blows meant for his son. The KGB would now concentrate on Viktor.

He wanted to know the real cause of death, but from the

moment the body arrived in Chuguyevka, the house was put under guard, day and night. No expert would be allowed in. In the end they consulted a surgeon who reviewed the facts. In deep secret he told them that the KGB had had Samuel poisoned. With great emphasis he adjured them: 'Don't tell anyone I told you, for then I won't ever see daylight again.'

They buried Samuel Walter on Sunday 21st October, one week after his mysterious death. The Russian name for Sunday is *Woskresenye*, which literally means 'Resurrection'. This day was a *Woskresenye* full of sorrow, and yet there was also a sense of expectation in the air. Snow fell and created a fairy-tale white world. Samuel lay in his casket as an honoured hero, as his sons carefully pushed it into the lorry platform. Ahead of the lorry children walked with garlands, while behind it six sons of Samuel carried the casket lid. About ten metres behind them a large crowd followed. Many songs were sung, hymns full of hope for every spectator who wanted to hear. They walked for about four miles, carefully watched by the KGB.

The KGB tried to protest that the cortege could have taken a shorter route, but the Chuguyevka Christians paid no attention to these murderers. They wanted everyone to hear them sing about eternal life and the grace of God. Some of the curious bystanders went along to the cemetery, wanting to witness a 'pentecostal funeral'. Perhaps they heard of God's love for the very first time, a short sermon was preached, and then all the family members kissed father Samuel farewell, one by one. Viktor stood at his head and continued to brush the snow off his father's face.

Everyone was deeply moved, except for two men who stared ahead without showing emotion and who didn't even take off their hats. They thought they had achieved victory, seeing only a body they had killed disappearing into the earth. They didn't understand the words which sounded like a shout of victory: 'For the wages of sin is death, but the gift of God is eternal life through Christ Jesus our Lord' (Romans 6:23).

After the funeral and the end of fasting all Chuguyevka Christians returned to their jobs. They had recovered enough and reported for duty to their old employers. But bitter disappointment awaited them. Except for a few women, all of them had lost their jobs. Their foremen were sorry, but there was no job left after a month of non-attendance. Some fellow workers protested, but soon held their tongues when they discovered that the superintendent had been pressured heavily by the KGB.

The Christians had no reserves and their only income consisted of revenue from the sale of forest products. In return for the assistance they themselves had provided for needy people near and far, they received some money or food once in a while.

But all the church members were agreed: the resistance of the past weeks was proof indeed that they were on the right road. Viktor said it once, 'We have to prepare for the most difficult times. It is written in 1 Peter 5:8: 'Your enemy the devil prowls around like a roaring lion looking for someone to devour.' Only if we remain faithful to God and each other, shall we not fall victim to the lion.'

They read the whole of Peter's first epistle once more, feeling that this apostle was addressing them directly: 'Dear friends, do not be surprised at the painful trial you are suffering, as if something strange were happening to you.' And, 'He will himself restore you and make you strong, firm and steadfast' (1 Peter 4:12 and 5:10).

'If the hunger strike got that much reaction and if we see how much stronger the attacks on our children have become, then we must not halt, but continue instead. All that the enemy desires clashes with what God desires. That makes the choice simple. When the atheists want to prohibit our services, children's worship and fasts, then it is God's will that we must continue with them.'

And so the whole congregation decided to go on hunger strike once more, beginning on 15th November. For them no grey existed any more, only black and white. The children of God were arrayed against the children of darkness, even though at this moment it looked as if the latter would gain victory.

15
The Flames Reach High

Chuguyevka, late 1984

After Samuel Walter's funeral the congregation grew more united than ever. The members used every chance to spend time together. They might have had reasons to be disheartened, but instead the air was full of good cheer. They even reserved time for fun. The meals had an especially festive character, with well prepared food and hours of conversation at the long tables.

A few days after the funeral, Pavel, Samuel's youngest son, had to report for military duty. Like his brothers, he could expect hard times, so a special worship service was arranged for him, and a generous farewell meal. Pavel had just turned eighteen and his father's loss had to be tougher on him than on his older brothers and sisters, who were already married. Everyone surrounded him with an extra measure of love, and some even accompanied him on the six-hundred-mile train trip to his base.

The local school had also been affected by the hunger strike stories and the events surrounding Samuel Walter. The administration and staff invited the KGB journalist, and a new article soon appeared. Its focus was the rights and duties of pentecostals. 'They want to leave for *die Heimat*, that depraved capitalist West Germany. But we have spent hundreds of thousands of roubles on their education and provided them with the world's best medical care. It hasn't cost them a cent. And now they want to just pack up and leave?' Clearly a matter of ingratitude, obvious theft when it comes down to it, the paper concluded. Of course the paper had not a word to say about the group's recent educational and medical experiences.

The article's purpose was simple: to cause a new campaign of troubles against the school children, thereby forcing the parents into another round of confrontation. In 1984 about eighty pentecostal children were attending school, a sizeable group whose impact could not be ignored.

Vladimir Walter's oldest son, eleven-year-old Pavel, came home with a bloody face, beaten up again. Vladimir went to see the principal. When he told him what had happened, the man shrugged his shoulders as if he couldn't do a thing about it. 'Well, Mr Walter, you know how boys are . . .' 'Of course I know!' said the indignant father, 'But your own colleagues saw that my son was brutally attacked. After they found out who the victim was, they merely turned away and pretended that nothing was going on. i know how boys are, and I also know that it's your responsibility to protect an eleven-year-old against the abuse of older boys. The day it happens again will be the last school day for all my children.' The principal swallowed hard at those blunt words, trembling with anger and almost choking on his response, 'I-i-i-f you do that, you'll lose your children, for we'll put them into a boarding school.'

A few days after this confrontation the third hunger strike began. For the greatest possible effect the Christians had attached posters to all their houses with the words: 'Third hunger strike.'

But the pressure on their school children kept increasing. The other students circulated the most outlandish tales, fed by the newspaper and their own teachers, about child sacrifices and other gruesome rituals which were supposed to take place inside the houses of the sectarians.

By the end of November 1984 the camel's back broke. Eight sets of parents wrote a letter to the school and school board, notifying them that they would keep their children at home.

One week later they were summoned, but as they were in the third week of fasting, they delegated Vladimir to go, and stayed home for their most important work: praying!

God was teaching them something unique. Their prayers were becoming more focused, their thoughts more pure. Even hot-tempered Tolya Sheludkov grew gentle and prayed earnestly for the kind of people he would probably have beaten up before. That's not to say that he wasn't very angry about the abusive treatment the children received. He thought that these KGB actions against small children were even more contemptible than the murder of Samuel, who after all was an adult.

Vladimir was told to have the children back in school the next day. All the parents could also expect judicial procedures aimed at relieving them of their parental authority. By the end of that day (6th December) Mr Drozdov, the public prosecutor, accompanied by a number of policemen, came to Viktor Walter's house to read them an official document with this last warning:

1. You must register your church.
2. All church members must take back their passports.
3. All the children must go back to school.

'If you ignore these demands, court procedures will begin', the man said.

9th December

On the following Sunday, the twenty-fourth day of the fast, they held a service at Valeri Lobsov's house. Everyone knew something was about to happen, for the authorities wouldn't rest until they had shown their naked power.

Halfway through the service the police arrived. Normally

they would hardly have noticed, but the police had no patience today, and instead of waiting for worship to end, they noisily entered. The choir began a hymn and the KGB agents began photographing all those present. No one was afraid, not even the children, used as they were to singing children's Christian songs even in the streets. They didn't mean to be defiant, but all the same they embarrassed the KGB and police alike. The children had no difficulty sensing the absurdity of the situation, the bravado and show of power of those adults who possessed so much devotion in combatting faith and Church.

After the service the servants of the law left for their homes, showing by their confident behaviour that judicial actions by Mr Drozdov, the public prosecutor, were close at hand.

10th December

Police jeeps and KGB cars began to arrive in Beregovaya Street by 10 o'clock the next morning. A large number of police officers and plenty of busybody men and women in plain clothes swarmed over the five pentecostal houses in that sweet, including Viktor Walter's. These houses, as well as other pentecostal houses elsewhere in Chuguyevka, were cordoned off. House searches resulted in Bibles, hymnals, personal documents and money being confiscated. The three houses the Christians had built along the river were searched especially closely. The officials tried to tear up Walter's floors, but solid construction resisted their attempts, and they gave up after a while.

The police at Valeri Lobsov's house became aggressive when Valeri clutched his Bible to his chest. An officer cruelly twisted his arm and snatched the book away. A female KGB agent forced his wife Yevgeniya to take her clothes off as their nine children watched with frightened eyes. After it was clear that she was hiding nothing, she was permitted to get dressed again. The police also behaved rudely at the house of Anatoli Khokha. Anatoli was still weak, weighing only eight and a half stone after his thirty day fast. For five hours they searched his house, while they forced him to remain standing, and then the KGB officer said, 'You're under arrest. Come along.' Anatoli fainted, but the man nodded to some police officers, who dragged the unconscious Christian to the waiting standard police prisoner van, nicknamed a 'Black Raven', which quickly took off for an unknown destination.

Vladimir Walter approached the officer in charge and asked, 'Could you show me your warrant?' The man barely looked up, and while leafing through one of the confiscated books, said, 'We have the power to hold you for three days without a warrant, so I'd keep my mouth shut if I were you.'

At about the same time Nikolai Vins was arrested and taken away. His wife firmly held the hand of their nine-year-old Harry, who had told the KGB agent who had arrested his Dad: 'You won't get my Dad, I'll lie down in front of your car.' Olga knew that her blond, blue-eyed Harry would do it.

More than fifteen houses were searched, keeping more than a hundred officials busy for about eight hours. Many Christian books and personal letters were taken from Viktor Walter. The most important items he had were copies of letters sent to Western government leaders. If they were found, this business could become a full-blown political scandal. Viktor had put the bundle of letters in an inside jacket pocket and slipped it casually to Mariya. Unfortunately, a KGB agent had spotted the move and tried to snatch them out of her hand. She was too quick for him and threw them to Peter Walter, who was immediately overpowered by three officers. While on the ground he managed to push the bundle to his wife Anna, who hid it underneath her blouse, unnoticed. The struggle with Peter took a bit of time before they discovered that he had nothing on him.

By six in the evening Viktor Walter's arrest became official. He demanded time to pray with his family. At first the police refused him, but Viktor stated, 'I know I won't see my family for a long time; you must allow it, for I am still master in my own house. In any case, I have to find some warm clothes for gaol.' A KGB agent said, 'But you'll be back home in three days.' 'I don't think so,' Viktor said, 'I know I'll be much longer, please don't tell me stories.' They finally allowed him his request, and the whole family entered the living room. Viktor, Mariya, Peter, Anna and all the children knelt down, while the police listened behind the closed door. Only people with hearts of stone could hear those prayers without shedding tears, but the KGB chief was just such a man. Unmoved he had the prisoner taken away a few moments later.

Outside, the police had cordoned off a path from front door to car, for they wanted to keep other Christians at a safe distance to prevent emotional scenes. All they could do was to call out. 'Viktor, be of good courage!' 'Viktor, you'll never be alone!' But not much could be said in such a few moments. The car left the street at great speed, far too fast for other brothers to follow.

Vladimir Walter arranged a special worship service that evening. The wives of the prisoners were the most concerned, of course. All the adults were present, except for the three prisoners and Gennadi Maydanyuk, who had left for Moscow a few days earlier to inform Western journalists of the tensions in Chuguyevka, and their decision not to send their children to school any more.

It proved to be an unusual evening. They had

experienced arrests before, even of the same men, but this was different. The air was full of threats and they expected more to happen. They felt that God was making clear that they could expect a long series of arrests. The congregation had not tried to avoid confrontations with the government. No one questioned their unyielding posture. Yet it was hard to come to grips with this new reality, especially for the women and children who had been left behind.

Remarkable things happened that evening. God used a number of members as channels of prophecy, of words of comfort, and of unfathomable wisdom. The love of God descended on this small and weak group of dependent human beings. He showed them that they would conquer. Viktor would be sentenced, and so would the others, but their victory was certain. God would lead them out of Chuguyevka in His way, a way they could not possibly imagine.

The prayers for Viktor, Nikolai and Anatoli were heartrending, and sure to be heard. God responded in clear words. He built up the faith of every one of them, and provided inner peace and unshakeable trust in the future. No one who was there ever forgot the hour of prayer on that Monday evening, 10th December. God placed before them a beacon of light that they would follow during the many dark months and years ahead.

Vladimir Walter, Yegor Betcher and Johan Vins began a search for the location of the prisoners. Drozdov, the local public prosecutor, denied that he knew where they were. Nobody would help them, so they travelled to the provincial court of justice in Vladivostok, where they learned that Viktor was indeed imprisoned there. However, no one knew where Vins and Khokha were. They arranged for some easily digestible food and broth, for Viktor was sure to become seriously ill on the usual prison food after his thirty-day fast. But when they reported to the prison, no one had heard of Viktor Walter. It was useless to stay around here, for they would simply be sent from pillar to post.

When they returned after three days, they discovered to their delight that Nikolai and Anatoli had been released for the moment, but that Viktor had disappeared without trace.

Without either knowing it, both Nikolai and Anatoli had been imprisoned in Arsenyev. That afternoon, after personal identity information had been recorded, they were abruptly put outside the prison. It was already dark when it happened to Nikolai. He had no money, and no coat or hat against the bitter cold. He made his way to the highway to see if he could catch a lift, but everyone seemed to pretend he wasn't there. After about fifteen minutes he spotted another hitchhiker. Nikolai looked at him closely and recognized Anatoli Khokha. They embraced, and strangely enough the first car after that stopped. The driver was willing to drive them all the way to Chuguyevka, for payment on arrival, a distance of more than fifty miles.

There was much rejoicing at their arrival, dampened a bit by the realization that no one knew Viktor's whereabouts.

Their uncertainty lasted until close to Christmas. They came to fear for the life of their pastor. After the death of Samuel they knew that the KGB would stop at nothing to get rid of Viktor. Time and time again the brothers visited the public prosecutor to ask for the whereabouts of Viktor, but they received no answer.

27th December

After almost two weeks without the slightest news, the congregation decided to hold a peaceful public protest. Two days after Christmas they visited the Chuguyevka court house. They had designed pamphlets that demanded both to know the whereabouts of Viktor Walter and the end to his illegal arrest.

It just so happened that a meeting of the 'Druzhiniki' (the much feared auxiliary police force) was underway at the police station next door. Mariya Walter and brothers Vladimir and Peter Walter entered the court house to present their demands to the public prosecutor. In the meantime the Christians were busy handing a pamphlet to every pedestrian. The police noticed their actions and quickly approached the demonstrators. 'Why are you here with so many people?' they asked Nikolai Vins, who was in charge of the street demonstration. He explained that Viktor Walter had disappeared since he had been arrested more than two weeks ago. 'We demand clear answers to two questions', he said while he handed a pamphlet over to the police. 'Where is our pastor being held, and will you let him go? It is illegal to hold someone for more than three days without due process.'

A police inspector went into the station to ask his superiors for advice. After fifteen minutes he returned with the demand that the Christians hand over all their pamphlets. 'No,' Johan Vins replied, 'we're not doing anything illegal, and we will provide information to everyone who is interested until our three delegates appear again with satisfactory answers to our questions. Then we'll depart.'

Two police officers grasped Johan Vins's arms and dragged him violently inside the police station. Next, they tried to rough up others. From the office of the prosecutor Vladimir and Peter saw what was happening. They left Mariya there and ran outside. Vladimir called, 'Hey, why are you doing that? Can't these people wait for an answer here? Mr Drozdov is busy calling Vladivostok, for we already know Viktor is a prisoner there, and we have a letter in our possession he himself wrote. Our first question has been answered already. Now we're asking for his release, and when we know the answer, we'll leave.'

But the chief of police yelled, 'No one may wait here. Go away, or we'll call for the army or the fire brigade with a water cannon.'

The Druzhiniki had come outside in the meantime and were prepared to attack. Their menacing posture made clear that they were itching to hand out solid beatings. It was also clear that they had been drinking freely at their meeting.

But the Christians did not want to provoke violence, and Nikolai Vins said, 'Okay, we'll go away, but not without my brother Johan. If you release him, we'll go.'

The prosecutor brought Mariya outside and told them that it would take two days for an answer from Vladivostok. 'That's fine,' Vladimir said, 'we'll go home. If you make sure that we are informed of the circumstances surrounding our pastor, then we don't need to demonstrate any more. But the police have taken Johan Vins away. We demand his instant release. Without him we won't go.'

The police remained unreasonable and ignored the demand of the demonstrators. Next the Druzhiniki were let loose, and a terrible fight ensued.

Two large brutes grabbed eleven-year-old Pavel Walter and began to beat and kick the child. Tolya Sheludkov spotted it and ran towards him. One of them was Sergeant Kavalchuk who had threatened Tolya with his pistol before Tolya's conversion. Tolya called out, 'Leave that child alone.' When they saw the giant forest worker approaching, they released Pavel, not knowing that Tolya wouldn't have touched them, for no Christian would defend himself. The Christians knew that the police were observing them closely to spot who would offer resistance, so that they could issue a complaint. The auxiliary police even beat and punched two pregnant women. Elvira Khokha had a miscarriage that day, and Olga Sheludkov's baby would be born prematurely and die after three weeks.

After this terrible end to a demonstration which had begun so peacefully, the police arrested nine men. Dejected, the others returned home. The only result they had achieved was the knowledge that Viktor was in a Vladivostok prison. The flames reached high into the sky that day. But for the fact that in the past God had spoken so clearly, as recently as the evening of Viktor's arrest, the fire might have been too searing for some.

16
The Shepherd Caged

Vladivostok, 11th December

At 4 a.m. the Lada in which Viktor Walter had been taken stopped in front of the KGB offices in Vladivostok. He had begun the trip sitting between two armed police officers like a dangerous criminal, but during the trip the tension eased. At one point they asked him, 'Who are you?' Viktor told them that he was a pentecostal pastor. 'But then someone has made a mistake. One hundred of us and fifteen cars were summoned for a dangerous mission involving a criminal gang.' 'Well,' Viktor said, 'that's how the KGB sees us, but in reality we're ordinary hard working people. Of course we believe in God the Creator and in his Son Jesus Christ Who has died for our sins.' The officers were astonished and wanted to know everything about those good tidings. Just before Vladivostok they said once more, 'This has to be a mistake. You'll be home again soon.' Viktor replied, 'I'm afraid not. If you knew what has been happening to us over the last few months, you'd understand that I may be locked up in a labour camp for years to come.'

Viktor was led inside and a guard prodded him along a hallway. He was at the end of his tether, twenty-six days into a hunger strike, exhausted by the house searches in Chuguyevka and the two hundred-mile trip without sleep.

They went down a set of stairs into a dank cellar, and through a long hall to a metal door. The guard looked through the shutter before he opened the door. The small stuffy room of only a few square yards reeked of stale sweat. It already contained a few other prisoners who didn't say a word. Viktor found the only available 'bed', a concrete ledge on which rested a few thin wooden boards. He stretched out and fell asleep.

For three days he wasn't aware of much more than his cellmates and the guard who brought in some thin soup twice a day. Viktor refused to eat. He hardly spoke with his fellow prisoners, who sat staring and showed no interest in him. Actually, Viktor had no need to talk and he wanted only to pray and think. He needed time to prepare himself spiritually for what was sure to come. He was convinced that the KGB wanted to break the congregation's resistance by isolating him, so that the members would lose courage.

On the fourth day Viktor was taken to the main Vladivostok prison. The back door of the Black Raven was driven right up to the entrance so that he wouldn't see anything. Roughly they pushed him outside the van, then through long halls with numerous doors. He lost all sense of direction. 'Look in front', his guard yelled if he dared to turn his head. The guard rattled his keys as he approached yet another door.

Finally they reached the door behind which Viktor would be locked up for an indeterminate time. The guard knew that Viktor could hardly stay on his feet, but he gave him a hard push that made Viktor tumble to the ground. Slowly he got up and crawled to the only available bunk. It had no mattress, and only an old dirty blanket, but he lay down straight away. He could barely stay on his feet because of the fasting.

One of the other three prisoners stood next to him and said, 'Who are you and why are you in here?' 'Sounds familiar', Viktor thought, seeing the other two approaching as well. 'I'm Viktor Walter and I'm here because I'm a Christian.'

'That's not what we heard. You've sacrificed children',

one of the others said. Viktor understood that the KGB had prepared them for his arrival. He told them his story, about their struggles with the authorities, and their third hunger strike to protest at the government taking their children away.

The three prisoners had seated themselves and listened attentively. Viktor didn't altogether trust them, but he had learned from previous prison experiences that honesty works miracles. After a while the oldest said, 'OK Viktor, we believe you. We'll talk again tomorrow.' He clearly was the leader, for the others kept quiet after that.

That night Viktor felt someone pulling his sleeve. The same man whispered in his ear, 'I respect you and know you speak the truth, but don't talk too much for the others work for *them*'

It turned out that he was an experienced criminal who was serving his fifth sentence. At first Viktor didn't know whom to trust, but he knew, deep in his heart, that God controls everything, even life in this horrid cell. The KGB kept bringing in new collaborators, but they all failed to influence Viktor or cause him ill. God continued to provide a 'guardian angel' in the form of a prisoner who supported him.

For his first few days in the giant Vladivostok prison Viktor was taken to a separate room to be interrogated, but he never responded and showed no co-operation. He grew too weak to stand on his legs and before too long they just left him in his cell. After his arrest Viktor continued his fast for another fourteen days. He grew so weak that he couldn't even sit on the edge of his bunk.

Yet he felt fine in all other respects. He had never been able to think so clearly. He had no headaches and wasn't dizzy. God showed him many things concerning His plan for the congregation, and about the spiritual background of these long struggles. Viktor saw most sharply that the efforts towards community and unquestioned obedience to God had driven Satan to mad anger.

He realized that at this moment every member of the community was being tested for endurance and faithfulness. The devil would attempt to drive wedges between members. Viktor concentrated on prayers, for every brother, every sister, every boy and every girl, even every little child. He had often preached about Jesus's personal attention and compassion for every individual, but never had he experienced this spirit of compassion in such a personal way as in that cell, far removed from close family and friends.

He was able to sustain prayer for hours, without becoming tired or repetitive. Remarkably, he no longer felt special love for his own wife and children, for he considered them brothers and sisters in Christ first of all. That change in his thinking made it possible for him not to be tortured by self-pity or family worries, even though he loved them dearly. His only care was for the purity and holiness of the Church of Jesus Christ. If the Chuguyevka congregation walked in God's ways, his family would fare well also. Actually, Viktor prayed for things he couldn't even comprehend. He simply became part of Jesus's caring for the congregation of which he was a pastor. So many hidden motives still remained: pride, greed, prejudices, unclean thoughts, hypocrisy, and other sins. The only things that would prevent the undermining of the congregation would be love, faithfulness and unquestioned obedience to the Word of God.

Viktor was convinced that his prayers got things on the move, that he actually was giving orders to angels who obediently executed them.

The KGB didn't know what to do with this Chuguyevka pastor. He clearly had his own agenda. He ate nothing, didn't leave his cell for fresh air, and answered not one of their questions. Even though he was captive, he seemed to continue to lead the congregation from Vladivostok. Worship services continued, the children were out of school and nobody withdrew emigration plans.

On exactly the fortieth day of his fasting (24th December), a KGB officer asked him to be so kind as to send a letter back home. 'Your friends in Chuguyevka are causing unrest in the whole world, and their protests about your disappearance have reached far across the border. Tell them to stop. Write them that you're well and still alive.' Those few phrases told Viktor enough: the congregation backed him to the hilt and had made the news of his arrest widely known. Now prayers from all over the world would be reaching God.

Viktor wrote his mother a brief note to ease her worry about him, but he refused to ask his brothers and sisters to stop their actions.

That Christmas Eve was a happy day for Viktor. The KGB information about life in Chuguyevka was an answer to his many prayers. The congregation was firmly anchored in the truth, and God would guard over every member. That evening Viktor sipped two spoons of fish soup, and a bit more of it every hour thereafter. After a few days strength slowly began to return to his muscles.

He also received a parcel, for as soon as the Chuguyevka people received his message, some set out for Vladivostok to bring him nutritious food and extra clothing.

But before Viktor could lay his hands on the parcel, the KGB examined every bit of its contents. Every piece of clothing received detailed examination, and all the food was ground to prevent any message from reaching him. But God provided yet one more miracle, for among the food bits Viktor found a small scrap of paper with six letters, enough to let him know that Anatoli Khokha and Nikolai Vins were free, and the congregation was united in holding fast to the faith and the vows they had made together.

The KGB tried everything it could to drive wedges between the members. As a predator from a distance chooses a weak animal, so they selected their victims. Over and over again the KGB threatened various members with arrest, if Viktor did not terminate his hunger strike.

That is why the peaceful demonstration on 27th December had been met with violence that had been the result of a carefully orchestrated operation intended to produce the largest possible number of arrests: Johan Vins first, then Valeri Lobsov, Yegor Betcher, Heinrich Walter, Yakov Dik, Leonard Voitke, Viktor and Benjamin Samsonov and Viktor Pavlovets.

A few months earlier Viktor Pavlovets had come to Chuguyevka to visit his sisters Mariya and Anna Walter. Ironically, he couldn't have chosen a worse moment, yet he had found the communal life so attractive, even in this time of great persecution, that he eagerly stayed and joined.

On 29th December, Peter Walter, married to Mariya's younger sister Anna, went to the Chuguyevka gaol to take some warm clothes for his brother-in-law Viktor Pavlovets. After he had reported (at the gate) and was ready to hand over the parcel, two KGB agents grabbed him. 'Terrific, that saves us the trouble of coming to get you', they said. Without ceremony they dragged Peter along and threw him into a cell.

After a few weeks the KGB made up its mind. The youngest prisoners, Viktor Pavlovets, Peter Walter and Viktor Samsonov, remained in gaol, while the others were released.

Viktor Samsonov celebrated his nineteenth birthday in gaol, on 16th January 1985. He was a quiet man, shy, but certainly not afraid. His courage was noticed by the criminals in gaol. When they learned that he had refused to join the army shortly before his arrest, this slender lad gained respect among some of them, and they protected him from the unsavoury prisoners who couldn't keep their hands off him.

Viktor Pavlovets was continually surrounded by informers. The KGB had gained a thorough dislike for this small redhead, who had outfoxed them before when they tried to entrap him and use him as an informer. Now he had to pay for that.

Peter Walter remained as stubborn and unyielding as his older brother Viktor. During the first interrogation he noticed that the words the KGB agent wrote down were different from what he had said. Peter asked the policeman who stood behind the agent, 'Would you check whether he wrote down what I said?' Surprised by this unusual request, the man reacted quite slowly. He looked down on the written text and discovered the discrepancy. The KGB was angry at the policeman, but even more at Peter, who added, 'If you don't record my answers literally, I won't answer at all.' His deeds were as good as his words, for he clamped his lips together and answered no more questions.

Furiously the interrogator yelled, 'I've worked here for twenty years and you're the first one to clam up!' In half an hour Peter was back in his cell, and he wasn't even summoned for a second interrogation.

The three of them were transported to Vladivostok on 20th January. With about a hundred prisoners they were herded into a cattle truck which was attached to a scheduled passenger train. They were together for the first time in three weeks, and the guards could not prevent them from sitting next to each other in that overloaded waggon. They used every minute to talk and pray together. The train arrived in Vladivostok at 6 a.m., and two hours later they entered the same gaol in which Viktor Walter was held.

That was the last time the three saw each other until their trial. Naturally, they asked the other prisoners whether they knew anything about Viktor Walter. No one knew, even though they had heard about the man who on his own had challenged the KGB and had begun two hunger strikes within one month.

Viktor Walter had indeed begun a hunger strike, on the day those three arrived. He knew nothing of the demonstration on 27th December, nor about the arrest of a number of church members and the three new arrivals. He was simply convinced that another period of fasting was required to force the KGB to abandon their war on Christians.

After he announced his hunger strike, Viktor was placed in a special, concrete cell. He had to take off all his clothes and was only given a striped, cotton prison uniform over his naked body. For his feet he had oversized shoes without laces. Day and night he froze in this isolation cell. During the day, from 5 a.m. to 9 p.m. his wooden bunk was chained up to the wall, but even when it was down Viktor couldn't sleep. The bunk was even smaller than normal, and he had no mattress or blanket. He had to keep moving so as not to freeze to death. As he weakened and lay still for longer periods, all feeling disappeared from his limbs. Finally, he couldn't stand up during the daytime either and he remained prone on the concrete floor.

Every day the KGB asked whether he wanted food. They demanded he write home with advice to give up the struggle and to give in to the three government demands: register the congregation, abandon emigration plans and return the children to school. But Viktor refused every time and was prepared to die.

'I'll never do what you ask. I'll never write a letter you'll dictate. And after this time in gaol I know our children have to leave. I won't need to emigrate. You can keep me here. I believe in God and I'm not afraid to die. But you'll leave my children alone and you won't have them to teach them your atheism.'

Every time Viktor told them that, the KGB officers slammed the iron door shut. They were furious and couldn't understand how this man, who never raised his voice and remained friendly, could so stubbornly hang on to his faith.

Actually, Viktor had given up hope that he would ever leave this terrible isolation cell alive. Yet after fourteen days of it, he was returned to an ordinary one.

17
The Gynaecologist

Chuguyevka, early 1985

The assault on the Chuguyevka Christians took on ever more evil proportions. Out of the window went observance of laws and regulations, however unjust even these might have been. A large number of people were blinded by their hate for the Christians, and members of the congregation met them at work, in hospitals, in schools and government offices. These people had drunk in that hate from their mother's breasts. They despised and paid little attention to ordinary Christians who meekly submitted to the authorities, but this pentecostal congregation seemed to mock their marxist utopia. More, it was humiliating to acknowledge that these simple workers seemed to practice Marxism, but out of their Christian faith instead. And yet this was the very faith that Marxists considered to be opium for the people, and the most massive example of fraud in human history.

Perhaps they didn't articulate all that to themselves, but the challenge of this pentecostal congregation seemed to drive them to crazy actions.

Elvira Khokha had a miscarriage as a result of the violence on 27th December. The KGB's influence reached right into the hospital. Through blackmail, doctors and nurses were forced to collaborate with them. After the birth of her dead child, Elvira was left alone, naked and bleeding heavily. If a nurse hadn't spotted her and taken care of her, she would surely have died.

Olga Sheludkova had received blows to her lower

abdomen and her baby was born prematurely. It died three weeks later. Tolya had been arrested just before this. Olga was summoned to the KGB offices where in the presence of the doctor she was threatened with arrest if she revealed the real reason for the death of her baby. 'We'll accuse you publicly of having sacrificed your child during a pentecostal worship ritual.'

The KGB had managed to get the whole hospital staff under its control. Elizabeth Voitke had to consult a gynaecologist. The doctor sent her into his office where she encountered a man who introduced himself as KGB agent Sergei Murashkin. He asked her to sign a paper in which she promised to become a regular KGB informer.

'I've come here to consult a doctor, but I'll leave it. I don't want to talk to you, and my family is waiting for me', was her response. The man began to threaten her with prison, but she refused to be intimidated. He let her go. He was known from that day on, by Christians and his colleagues both, as 'the gynaecologist'.

The next day Elizabeth returned to the doctor's office, with her husband Leonard. 'Why do you turn this hospital into a KGB recruitment office?' they asked. Startled, the physician reacted, 'Please don't ask such questions. That's the way things are and they are not likely to change.'

Faith in the medical profession was already low after the death of Samuel Walter, but experiences such as these made visits to the hospital life-threatening.

The last hospital visit by a Chuguyevka pentecostal Christian took place in early March 1985. Anna Walter, Vladimir's wife, gave birth to her ninth child there, and everything seemed normal until a doctor visited her and said, 'There's something wrong with your child.' Anna was frightened, for she had already seen Rudolph and he seemed to her as healthy and normal as her other eight. Though scared, she said, 'I don't believe you. Rudolph is normal, and if there's something wrong with him now, you've caused it. I remember my father-in-law.'

The doctor replied, 'How can you say that, Mrs Walter? Why don't you go home, and we'll keep the baby here for a while, in an incubator.' Anna refused and telephoned Vladimir to pick her up right away.

All the church members were contacted that day to pray and fast. They feared the worst for Anna and her baby. In the meantime, a nurse approached Anna when she was alone. 'Let me show you something', she said seriously, looking around to see whether anyone was watching them. She took Anna to the incubator with little Rudolph inside, and pointed to the baby's right hand before leaving Anna alone. The little hand trembled violently and was blue with the marks of injection needles.

When Vladimir arrived they both immediately sought out the doctor. They asked him bluntly, 'Is this KGB work?' 'No, why do you think that?' the physician responded, clearly ill at ease. While they talked, his assistant entered to tell him there was a telephone call for him, but he said, 'I'm busy. I'll call back.'

The assistant returned, however. Clearly embarrassed, she said, 'Doctor, I'm sorry, it's urgent. It's Mr Samburov.' Vladimir knew him well, as he was one of the three top KGB officers in Primorski. He said, 'Now I know the truth, doctor. Come along, Anna, we'd better get out of here quickly.' They rose and left, and at the door Vladimir added, 'Doctor, if anything happens to our child, the whole world will be told.' Behind their back they heard the doctor berate his assistant for having dropped the KGB officer's name.

Rudolph recovered quickly, although he experienced a slight paralysis in his right hand for the rest of his life.

That was the day the Christians decided not to consult doctors or the hospital any more. Lyudmila Teplikh had been a hospital nurse before, and had worked in the maternity ward until she (and all the other Christians) had been fired. She now became a private nurse and midwife in the community.

For all the sick in the congregation, the elders would first be called to lay their hands on the patients and anoint them with oil, as described in the Bible. From that day on the number of faith healings increased dramatically in this community of about a hundred children and almost sixty adults, with its regular quota of illnesses. To this day they have no way of knowing which serious and less serious illnesses were healed among them, as they had no doctor to provide official diagnoses.

But healing was more important than diagnosis, and God provided miracle healings of illnesses time and time again. God also blessed the hands of Lyudmila to provide blessings for both pregnant mothers and their babies.

Ella, the wife of Johan Vins, had not come to faith in all this time. She would quietly listen to the stories which told of the need for repentance and confession of sins, but she didn't think those were needs she had. She thought, 'I know God exists. Why then worry about all this? I live a decent life and look after my husband and children.'

But these miracle healings of so many adults and children made her think again. She contemplated, 'If God heals the sick as it says in the Bible, then the other promises found in the Bible must be true too. That means He gives me eternal life if I believe in Him.' Ella told Johan that she wanted to accept Jesus as her Lord and Saviour. She prayed with the elders, confessed that she had been proud and stubborn, and repented. She was baptized in the Ussuri river on 21st July 1985.

Vladivostok, January/February 1985

Before this celebration of baptism a lot of things had happened in both Chuguyevka and Vladivostok.

After the KGB gave up trying to force Viktor Walter to change his mind, he abandoned his hunger strike on 30th January. He hadn't eaten anything for two weeks, and had almost frozen to death in his concrete cell, yet the KGB and not he had lost the battle. On the face of it he had stood alone against that powerful secret service, but in reality he had been surrounded by God's army of praying people and angels.

Viktor's fasting gained him insight in the spiritual battle he waged. After every daily KGB visit he had to resist feelings of loneliness. The KGB kept telling him that he had been forgotten, and that he was the very last one to continue his resistance. He knew it wasn't true, but these were the only words he heard. In fact, all letters and parcels for him were intercepted. For a long time he didn't even know that Peter Walter, his brother-in-law Viktor Pavlovets and Viktor Samsonov were prisoners in the same complex.

Chuguyevka, February

The same war raged in Chuguyevka. The very day that Viktor abandoned his own hunger strike in gaol, the community began another one, which lasted from 1st February to 1st March. New posters were attached to the houses which stated the reason for the fast, namely the right of every Soviet citizen to emigrate. The police fell all over themselves removing the posters. As a joke one of the brothers had painted the same words on the wooden façade of his house, and the police needed a quick can of paint to remove them.

The regional government reacted furiously to this fourth hunger strike. Three deacons, Nikolai Vins, Anatoli Khokha and Gennadi Maydanyuk, were arrested on 26th February, and sentenced that very day to one year of labour camp for the 'crime' of travelling everywhere without a valid passport. For instance, Maydanyuk had been in Moscow for contacts with Western journalists. For the time being the prisoners were kept in the Vladivostok prison, because there the KGB was preparing its case against Viktor Walter and the other three prisoners.

On 1st March three more brothers were arrested: Bernhard Rosher, the deacon, Oleg Lobanov, the photographer and film maker whose materials were already circulating in the West, and Tolya Sheludkov, the first Chuguyevka convert.

They too were transported to the Vladivostok gaol, where a total of ten now resided. Each of them was placed in a separate cell so that no contact between them was possible.

Vladivostok, March

In spite of the strictly enforced separation of the ten prisoners, they managed to receive some information about each other. The other convicts were adept at inventing new ways of keeping in touch. The sewers became a postal delivery system: letters were transported from cell to cell and fished out of the stinking pipes. With the exception of some prisoners who had sold their services to the KGB, every prisoner lent a hand. Anyone who had to consult the doctor looked behind the heating and the baseboards of the doctor's waiting room for any hidden letters. If the letter was for someone else, he memorized its contents and put it back.

Soon enough the whole gaol knew that it contained ten

Christians from the same church. Within a few days even the cell numbers were known. However, personal encounters in this four-thousand-inmate institution were impossible to arrange. Most promising were chance encounters in the exercise hall, when thirty-five to forty prisoners were permitted to walk around for an hour underneath air ducts in the roof. Each prison wing had seven of these halls, separated by walls about ten feet high. On top of heavy bars that served to prevent escapes, armed guards walked up and down. When it seemed safe, one of the prisoners would kick against the wall to let the others know the number of his cell. If a response from an acquaintance came from a neighbouring hall, the two would try to place themselves on each side of a weak spot in the wall.

With four thousand prisoners, the chance that friends would be in adjoining halls was rare, and that's why the brothers also made this situation a topic of prayer for a miracle. Nikolai Vins and Viktor Walter had to wait for about a month, but Nikolai could hardly hide his joy when he heard the number of Viktor's cell: two-two-four. One of his cellmates watched the guards while a conversation took place, watchful of a signal to stop. They managed to exchange some crucial information during that hour. Nikolai learned that Viktor was to be tried in early April and would probably face a five-year sentence. Nikolai told Viktor that the congregation had gone on hunger strike again and that he, Khokha and Maydanyuk had been sentenced to one year in a labour camp.

However, Nikolai didn't even know that Anatoli and Gennadi had already left for labour camps close to Vladivostok. Gennadi went to Galenki, close to the Chinese border. The camp was located about sixty-five miles west and houses about two thousand five hundred prisoners. The special KGB unit, formed at Galenki to combat the

Chuguyevka Christians, used every opportunity to force him to collaborate, and when he refused he was severely punished. Yet he remained as stubborn as the rest and wouldn't let himself be intimidated.

Anatoli Khokha was transported to a labour camp east of Vladivostok, where he received the same 'preferential treatment' by the KGB. He too resisted all their frantic efforts, and even when they threatened to withhold him the legitimate visits by his wife, he wouldn't budge. Better no visits than being a traitor.

The prisoners themselves made a sharp distinction between principled people and those who collaborated with the KGB, as the following story from Tolya Sheludkov made clear. It happened shortly after his arrival in the Vladivostok jail on 1st March 1985.

'When they opened the door of my cell, I saw that there really was no room for me, so I kept standing. A guard with a dog approached me, and he slowly released the dog's leash. Barking wildly, the monster sprang at my legs, and whether I wanted to or not, I had to enter the cell. One of the prisoners moved over a bit and I could wedge myself between him and another one.

'Before anyone said a word, I said, "I'm a Christian; I believe in God and pray to Him daily. I'm Anatoli Sheludkov from Chuguyevka."

'"Got your drift", said his neighbour, who introduced himself. The ice was broken and I received no opposition. The other prisoners had used an iron bar that had been smuggled inside to force a peephole in the iron plate before the window. "Why don't you pray there," they said, "then you won't bother us." I gratefully followed their suggestion. I could look out on the Vladivostok harbour and found the spot ideal for prayers. After a few weeks the guards discovered the hole and welded it shut again, but they never found the steel bar, even after thorough searches.

'Another prisoner joined us, a young man of about twenty. The moment I saw him I was convinced that the KGB had instructed him to spy on me.

'I made the mistake of sharing my conclusion with the other prisoners, big brutes with tattoos on their chests and arms. They immediately began to harass the newcomer, and I was sorry I had let it slip out.

'The next day the newcomer was taken away, and after an hour he returned with tea, which was after drugs the most sought-after commodity in the "Gulag Archipelago". That clinched the matter, and my protectors grabbed him in order to rape him. I jumped in between then and told them I could look after myself, seeing that he was placed here to spy on me. I was happy that they abandoned their intentions, but later I heard them whisper about killing him at night. I knew they would do it, for I had experienced the same thing with non-Christian prisoners before. I prayed for a solution, and just before curfew the KGB removed him.'

18
In Court

Chuguyevka, April 1985

The date for Viktor Walter's court case in Chuguyevka was 2nd April 1985. The unfortunate judge was Valeri Mikhailyukov, himself a prisoner of his own conscience, who for seven days had to adjudicate a case which had been decided in advance. He was caught between sentencing Viktor Walter to five years in a labour camp or a confrontation with the KGB.

A number of church members, mainly family, had been admitted to the courtroom. However, most of the spectators were *komsomol* youth with their teachers, as this court case against the pentecostal leader was part of their curriculum. The court house was surrounded by an unusually large number of policemen, and a large number of police and soldiers were inside as well. Flanking the accused on the first row were heavily armed soldiers.

During the last day of the case, 11th April 1985, the history of Pilate, and of his wife who had dreamed of Jesus, was echoed in the courtroom. One of the two women jurors began to protest against the severe sentence, and the judge's self-control wavered. Blushing, Valeri Mikhailyukov bent over to her and said, quietly so that no one else would hear: 'I would rather acquit him. A year ago I had a nightmare about this and another case, in which it was prophesied that I would convict innocent people because of their faith. But what can I do? I've got my instructions, I have to sentence him to five years or I'll be in deep trouble.' (After the court case the same juror told this story to Frida, Viktor Walter's mother.)

The judge asked Viktor whether he had anything to say for himself. Viktor rose and said, 'It is a great honour for me to be pastor of this congregation, and I feel that God has blessed me. I am no criminal and I'm happy to suffer for the name of Christ Jesus.'

After the reading of the sentence, flowers rained down upon the court room. The soldiers in the front row didn't realize what was happening and dived to the floor. With gusto all the Christians began to sing a hymn about the Church of Jesus Christ which conquers, from Nero's time to the last day. An officer called out, 'Quick, quick, take him outside.' The soldiers dragged Viktor through the aisle while the other Christians continued singing.

Some *komsomol* members were indignant about the sentence and said, 'That man has been sentenced to five years on the basis of no more than a few vague accusations. No one offered any proof.'

Between the door of the court house and the waiting Black Raven an impenetrable wall of soldiers and policemen stood at the ready. It was their job to prevent any contact between Viktor and his family and friends. When his daughter Anna saw her father, she quickly crawled through all the legs, and before any one could stop her, she pushed a chocolate bar into his hands. 'Daddy', her high voice sounded out. More she couldn't say for she was roughly grabbed by a soldier who threw her back over the wall of uniforms. Another soldier snatched the chocolate from Viktor's hand and stomped on it with his boots, as if possessed and in need of personal revenge.

Viktor had difficulty in not crying. He had made a vow never to show his emotions in the presence of the KGB and other enemies. Of course he had his weak moments, but they wouldn't know that, ever. Their hatred was so intense that they were always looking for a weak spot to exploit to their advantage.

Viktor was brought to the police station in Chuguyevka, where he met the local police chief, Dobish. The man was sad, and said, 'Mr Walter, none of this is my doing, but only KGB work. I had never expected this, five years! I'll do my best to help you.' The man kept his word and regularly looked after sending parcels and letters.

Viktor was kept in the Arsenyev prison for another week, where he celebrated his first Easter in prison. From Arsenyev they brought him back to the Vladivostok prison.

On 21st April the trial against the seven remaining prisoners began, also in the Chuguyevka court house. Judge Valeri Mikhailyukov had dreamed of two cases, and he got two . . . two within one month.

For every person with any sense of justice this case also became a travesty. The seven brothers sat next to each other in the dock, sad in the knowledge that their sentence was already fixed while the trial was still in progress. This violation of law, this show case, was a mockery. Almost a whole day was spent interviewing witnesses who claimed to have been beaten up by specific brothers on 27th December 1984, but when the judge asked them to point these out to him, they would look around as if to say, 'I thought we wouldn't be asked difficult questions.'

Had the circumstances not been so serious, the whole trial would have been laughable. But the judge didn't laugh when he handed out the following sentences: Nikolai Vins, five years in labour camp; Peter Walter, four years; Viktor Pavlovets, four and a half years; Viktor Samsonov, three years; Bernhard Rosher, four years; Oleg Lobanov, three and a half years; Tolya Sheludkov, five years' hard labour.

The congregation threw flowers once more and sang a hymn. The prosecutor wanted to stop it, but the unhappy judge lift d his tired head and said, 'Let them be, they're not doing any damage.'

The seven convicts were brought back to Vladivostok

where they had to wait for transport to the labour camps. Because the labour camp administration is based in Moscow, it took months before they left Vladivostok. They were still carefully kept apart and continually harassed by the KGB, whose long, controlling arms continued to reach into their very cells.

19
A Traitor Unmasked

In the summer of 1985, the KGB thought up a new ploy to get rid of Viktor Walter. He was regularly moved from one cell to another, sometimes more than once a week. After two moves he caught on to their plans. Veteran criminals already knew that prisoners who frequently changed cells were collaborators. According to the prisoners' unwritten code, such a traitor would be the recipient of severe punishment. Rumours of collaboration began to swirl around Viktor, and the Chuguyevka congregation decided to begin fasting again. Only their prayers could help Viktor and the other prisoners. This fifth fast lasted from 25th July to 5th August.

God answered their prayers in a most unexpected way and the satanic plans of the KGB failed completely. The guards executed their orders to perfection, and Viktor went from cell to cell, but they had overlooked the rule of not allowing two Chuguyevka prisoners in the same cell. Viktor had prayed earnestly to God for a meeting with one of the brothers, and God used the KGB for an answer to his prayers.

The first 'mistake' was made immediately after the court case, when Viktor Pavolvets was 'accidentally' placed in the cell of his pastor. The two men couldn't believe their eyes! This error was an undoubted miracle in that prison with four thousand convicts. But that wasn't all. They discovered that Bernhard Rosher was in the adjoining cell.

Pastor Viktor Walter had especially prayed for these two.

Viktor Pavlovets had moved to Chuguyevka only a few months before, and he feared that Bernhard's sensitive nature might not be able to withstand the inhuman cruelties of this prison. But now he could communicate with both, and they could encourage each other. Contact with Bernhard was maintained through the 'sewer mail', a piece of paper attached to a wire which was wriggled next door through the toilet hole in the floor.

Viktor wrote a moving letter about this contact with some of these brothers, shortly before he was transported to the labour camp.

'You will have heard already that I was moved from one cell to another so that I'd be suspect, but their plans failed, and the Lord has used me for His own plans, with a miracle one could barely imagine in this environment. I've made contact with all seven! How much I had prayed for that to happen. My heart troubled and I worried for them.

'Peter and I were in one cell together for fifteen days and Tolya was in the next one. It still wasn't easy to talk to Tolya, so most of our "conversations" were in writing, but I also saw his face three times. What shall I say about them? Both Peter and Tolya surpassed my wildest expectations. I was overjoyed to learn that both were prepared to die for the truth of the Gospel.

'After a while the prison authorities discovered their "mistake", and I was moved to another cell. Peter cried at our parting, and I was sad too, but when I entered my new cell, my sorrow changed to great joy, for there sat Oleg Lobanov!

'Right then I was reminded of a talk with Peter, a few days before, in which we had mentioned how nice it would be also to have contact with Oleg Lobanov and Nikolai Vins. Here my desire was granted. Oleg knew how to reach Nikolai in writing, and a lively correspondence developed with him. Oleg had changed, and has become a devoted and powerful disciple of Jesus!

'Around that time I also saw Nikolai in person, not even alone but with Peter and Tolya! Their faces shone, and when they saw me, Nikolai boldly called out, "Greetings, brother!" My heart almost burst with joy and I couldn't hold back my tears when I saw those brave soldiers of God walk there.

'Before and after the trial I prayed much for Viktor Pavlovets and Bernhard. Viktor was such a novice, and Bernhard − or so I thought − needed so much teaching. I desperately tried to make contact with them myself, but without result. What a joy when Viktor was placed in my cell after the trial. Bernhard was nearby, behind the wall. Viktor and I talked a lot, and I stood amazed at his wisdom. he said, 'I'm grateful that I joined the congregation just in time. What would have become of me in Krasnodar? I am privileged to suffer for the work and Church of God, as my father Andrei did.' Contact with Bernhard was in writing only, but our hearts were one, and for God's Word walls do not exist!

'Victor Samsonov has a powerful faith for one so young. I talked to him when we both received visitors from Chuguyevka. Both before and after the visit I was able to exchange a few words with him, but you'll know that already from the visitors.

'These miracle meetings were part of God's plan. I now know that all seven are standing fast in the faith, and not only they, but you also. Of course the brothers have told me all about the enormous efforts and dedication of the entire congregation after my arrest, and how you cling together as a close family, entirely according to the Scriptures.'

KGB tactics were only partially successful. Beyond the miraculous meetings with the seven brothers, Viktor was able to talk about his faith with many criminals. Dozens of underworld figures, murderers, and even those who had received the death penalty, heard the Gospel for the first time in their lives. They proved very receptive, and more than one of them repented. Viktor taught them spiritual songs and even other prisoners would join in the singing.

Towards the end of his 'journey' through the Vladivostok prison, Viktor was locked up with three dangerous criminals. One was a clever but thoroughly evil man, who worked for the KGB and was adept at spreading the kind of rumours that cause dissension. The other two were large, strong and ignorant. Viktor immediately sensed the KGB agent and realized that he was in great personal danger.

The little man obviously felt powerful in the protection of the KGB. Viktor took him aside and told him, 'Listen, I know you work for the KGB. If you touch me, I'll make sure the whole Gulag Archipelago knows, and you know what that means: you'll be killed some day in some labour camp.'

The man paled, powerless against this measured approach. A few moments earlier his KGB link had made him feel secure, but now panic seized him. He whispered, 'I know you're right. Tomorrow I've got to tell them what happened here today. This is my fifth stint in gaol and they've promised me the world if I collaborate. I don't know how to get out from under them.'

Viktor couldn't know whether he meant what he said. He had already learned that this type would tell the most convincing tales, and then betray you.

The next morning the KGB informant was indeed taken from the cell. Within half an hour he returned, with a bag of groceries. Next, Viktor was taken away for an interrogation by two KGB agents he had met before. When Viktor returned he saw the two other prisoners staring ahead. The KGB collaborator told him he had given them drugs the KGB had provided.

It almost looked as if he considered Viktor his father confessor, for he told him, 'I have to arrange for a fight between you and those two, in any way I can. They have promised me an immediate release from my three-year sentence if they murder you in this cell. They'll even get me a flat in Leningrad or Moscow. The drugs will help me control their actions, but I won't do it. I know you're right: sooner or later other prisoners will kill me. They'll find me even in Moscow.'

On the very day Viktor was due to be murdered, the whole prison was informed via the 'sewage mail': 'If anyone as much as touches Chuguyevka prisoner Viktor Walter, he'll pay the price.' The 'letter' that reached Viktor's cell was signed by Valentin Protasov, himself a condemned murderer.

Viktor's companions looked at him wide-eyed. 'Who are you, that Protasov would protect you?' Viktor had never met this hard man face to face, but they had been in adjoining cells once, and Viktor had used the sewer to tell him about God. He was twenty-six years old, a righteous man who had murdered an infamous KGB stool-pigeon in one of the labour camps. All the prisoners respected him deeply, for he had shown no fear in defending the weak. When Viktor talked to him, he was living in great fear of his coming death, and he wanted to know everything about eternal life and forgiveness of sins.

Protasov's letter resulted in a more peaceful life for Viktor, and the little traitor was transferred to another cell.

Back in Chuguyevka, the remaining members worked even harder than before. The ten men now in prison and labour camp represented a severe loss. The absence of wages made the job of providing for a hundred and seventy members very difficult. God provided a rich vegetable and potato harvest, and the forest also yielded profitable products. Even with all those blessings, however, food was scarce: and yet no one complained. Being one large family, they would survive the winter. They had no doubts about that. The families of the ten prisoners were even given a bit more than the others, for the food distribution counted the prisoners in as still present. On top of that, the best was reserved for those prisoners and given to them on visits.

They spared no effort and expense to visit the ten, wherever they were. Vladimir Walter managed to visit his brother Viktor in August. Of course they could only talk in the presence of a guard. Vladimir had not come alone. Outside four other brothers waited. They had hatched a plan, and Walter was to present it to Viktor. During the two hours of visiting Walter was unable to present the plan without the guard hearing it too. He turned to the man and asked, 'Could we sing a farewell hymn to all our brothers in this prison? I think they'll hear it from the road behind the prison.' The guard shrugged his shoulders and replied, 'Go ahead, I don't think anyone will hear it from there anyway.'

The two brothers said goodbye. At the appointed time the five drove to the road, where they first prayed that all prisoners would hear their songs. The wind would blow the sound to the prison, although unfortunately a heavy machine working nearby threatened to overpower the songs.

But they couldn't wait any longer. And their prayers were heard, for exactly at the right time something went wrong with the machine, and its engine stopped for repairs. The operator climbed down, muttering under his breath, and the other labourers crowded around the machine. All of them clearly heard the beautiful music bounce off the walls of the prison.

The words were clear, previously recorded on cassette tape and broadcast with the help of a strong amplifier. After the hymns, Yegor Betcher recited a beautiful poem, which

touched all the prisoners, not only his spiritual brothers,
deep in their hearts.

Wherever a storm of unbelief blows,
a hurricane batters the sanctuary,
then listen, church, your Saviour calls,
his voice like lightning through the sky.

Oh wretched person on whom this deluge descends,
you are being tested by these storms and struggles.
But love, gained in exile,
will conquer with its superior strength.

Joy of my Spirit,
you have grasped the calling of the Bride.
That's why we travel this road together,
this road that began in Golgotha.

And when you are torn from your loved ones,
because of the sentence they gave you,
I'm still with you in the Black Raven,
and behind barbed wire fences too.

My name wasn't mentioned at roll call,
neither yesterday or today,
Yet in your suffering I'm as close to you,
as the breaking waves are to the beach.

I too work in the stone quarry, like you,
I too work in the sawmill, like you.
I rejoice: your spirit has not been crushed,
you shore up your words with your deeds.

When you bed down on your bunk,
I kneel at your head and behold your face.

The whole night My love surrounds you,
together we greet the morning.

Beloved, endure yet a little while,
do not weep because of sorrow and pain.
I am coming, I stand at the gate already,
and triumphantly I welcome you into My Kingdom.

Not until the last few lines did the KGB spring into action.
The brothers drove away quickly and managed to lose their
pursuers on a small country road.

They could not be sure whether their brothers behind
bars had heard the songs and poem, but they were
convinced they had done the right thing. If nothing else,
the KGB would hear that their victims would never be
forgotten.

But the message had reached the prison. Most of the
prisoners talked about it. Not all eight had heard it
personally, but from all sides they heard: 'You've got
terrific friends. They risked arrest to let you know you have
not been forgotten.'

Shortly afterwards, seven of them were spread out in
labour camps all over the Soviet Union. Viktor Pavlovets
was the only one who stayed in Primorski, in an infamous
camp four miles to the east of Chuguyevka. Viktor
Samsonov and Bernard Rosher were sent to two separate
Central Asian camps. On 20th August Nikolai Vins, Peter
Walter, Tolya Sheludkov and Oleg Lobanov were put on
the same train, destination Khabarovsk, almost five
hundred miles north of Vladivostok. They spent the whole
day together, and used every moment to share experiences
and encourage each other for the coming ordeals.

Viktor Walter was the last one to leave. On 12th
September he was put on a train to Arkhangelsk, in the far,
far north.

Nikolai later told the story of his own transportation, which brought him to a camp at the Kaspian Sea, seven thousand five hundred miles away.

'On the platform in Khabarovsk I immediately spotted Peter, and I yelled out that I was going to Krasnovodsk. They pushed him into the same train, but in another carriage. "Krasnoyarsk!" I heard him call out, which meant a further twelve hundred and fifty miles in the same direction.

'A little bit later I also saw Tolya on the platform. As I saw him looking around I yelled out, "Tolya, here". He spotted me and yelled back: "Tyumen." At the same time I heard Oleg's voice from the other side of the platform, "Lensk, Yakutsk". It was clear that we were to be kept apart as far as possible.

'They pushed us inside and closed the door. It took four days to reach Irkutsk, the end of the second leg. There we stayed in prison for a week, overrun by lice, mosquitoes and complaining prisoners. Thirteen days after our departure they brought me to Novisibirsk, three days away. There I stayed in a crowded prison for another two weeks. After a month of travel I was still only halfway. How much longer? When could I send a letter home?

'On the thirtieth day I departed for Tashkent, another four-day trip and another fifteen-day stay in prison. My mind was on my friends in the pentecostal congregations of Tashkent and in Akhangaran; they were so close by, but I was only a number, stripped of my rights, and the idea of talking to them could only be an illusion.

'The trip between Tashkent and Askhabad took another two days on a freight train. In Askhabad, close to the Iranian border, I spent twenty days waiting for final transport, in an unbearably hot prison even this late in October. And then to think that in Chuguyevka it would already freeze about ten degrees. The other Askhabad prisoners told me what my destination would be. Krasnowodsk had two camps, one for "ordinary" criminals and one for drug addicts and members of organized crime families. I would be placed in the latter, they told me. In Askhabad I was able to talk about my faith honestly and openly. One of the prisoners left for the same camp a few days before me and he promised to let the other prisoners know of my coming.

'Exactly seventy-five days after my departure I arrived at the labour camp of Dzhanga, a few miles north of Krasnovodsk. Looking through the bars at the back of the lorry at 4.00 a.m., I saw how the gates were closed behind me, and I realized that here I would live, sleep, work for a few years . . . as well as suffer.

'Dzhanga was a "black camp", meaning that the day-to-day organization was in the hands of prisoners, who were supervised by the "reds", the communists. My "herald" had informed the foremen of my coming. One of them approached me and brusquely asked, "And who are you?" I told him my name, and immediately his attitude improved. He stuck out his hand and said, "Nikolai Vins? Don't worry, you've got friends here."

'After finding a bunk in the barracks, I was summoned to the KGB office. The officer read through my files and said, "Nikolai Vins? From Chuguyevka? You've got a five-year sentence. Don't even think of preaching your propaganda here, for we'll add another five years if you do."

'I was exhausted after my long trip, but God always provides strength in the face of these bullies. He reminded me that I could hold my head without shame. I looked the man straight in the eye and said, "You just listen, mister. I've got five years and that's all. I must do what God commands me to do: Go out and proclaim the Gospel. And what do you want me to say when other prisoners ask me why I'm here? I can only tell them it is because of my faith.

And I'll tell them that I want to emigrate because you want to steal my children.' The KGB officer stared back at me in amazement, and angrily retorted, 'If that's so, we'll lock you up in solitary, and that'll be the end of your preaching."

'I told him, "Do what you have to do, and we'll see. You don't scare me. God is in charge."

'This place was no different from the other prisons: I remained a KGB target and a friend of prisoners.'

20
Ten Missionaries

The Chuguyevka congregation had only one central objective for its move to the east coast province: mission. For more freedom, a move to the Baltic states would have been better. But Primorski was a province where the Gospel had not yet been preached.

Their congregation constituted the first organized mission effort in this region. Within a few years it produced five mission posts within a radius of a hundred and twenty-five miles.

Even in the difficult years after the arrest of Viktor Walter and the others, mission work continued. The congregation considered the prisoners as a type of missionary sent out for an extraordinary type of service within the framework of the Great Commission. That understanding was reflected in the words of Nikolai to the KGB man on his arrival in the labour camp: 'I have to do what the Word of God tells me to, "Go out into the world and proclaim the Gospel."'

In the labour camps millions of people longed for the message of redemption and salvation in Jesus Christ. No statistics are available about the Gulag Archipelago, but it is estimated that the twenty million forced labourers form the least penetrated mission fields in the world. Yet the few 'missionaries' in it are among the best. They have no theological or pastoral training, but they are prepared to give their own lives for the Kingdom of God.

All the members of the Chuguyevka congregation knew

that they were in danger of being persecuted for their choice of the radical lifestyle which had begun to blossom in Akhangaran. Some had made the choice only a little time before their arrest, and others a long time ago, but no one had been surprised by imprisonment. Their spiritual training prepared them for persecution to begin any day. They sought a constant personal relationship with God, and also the communion of saints: discuss everything together, confess all sins, be receptive to being admonished and, especially, join fasts and prayers. Of course the ten missionaries in the Gulag Archipelago were isolated, but their firm conviction about still belonging to the Church made them feel peaceful and prepared. It made them focus less on themselves and more on 'the Great Commission'. In these camps the fields were ripe for the harvest and they had an opportunity to reach thousands with the Gospel.

The camp authorities tried everything to prevent the ten from talking, but God Himself had taken charge of this unique mission project. No matter how heavy the punishment, God kept opening new doors. The experiences of Tolya Sheludkov, Nikolai Vins and Peter Walter were typical.

Tolya Sheludkov had not been a Christian for all that long, but he knew Jesus had said: '(My Father) cuts off every branch in me that bears no fruit, while every branch that does bear fruit he prunes, so that it will be even more fruitful' (John 1:2).

Tolya had received a sentence of five years' hard labour, and had been sent to a special camp for recidivists. Across each page of his dossier a thick red line had been drawn, indicating the need for harsh treatment.

Immediately after his arrival the KGB interrogated him. 'If you mention God, we'll let you rot in solitary', they said. But Tolya replied, 'If a prisoner asks me about my faith, I'll answer. So, if you want to shut me up, make sure no one asks. Perhaps you should warn the camp on the loudspeakers.'

'You've got to be kidding,' the KGB officer said, 'that would be a good way of letting them all know that you are an evangelist. There's only one spot for you: solitary.' Tolya retorted, 'I can't keep quiet about my faith. My faith is as important as my food. I can't live physically without bread, but without talking about God I die spiritually.'

The labour camp consisted of two sections which were forbidden to communicate with each other. Nevertheless, Tolya regularly managed to cross the border between the two. The camp only had about five hundred prisoners, and soon everyone knew him. Because of his many contacts with prisoners, guards, and even with people outside the camp, he managed to smuggle inside a Bible, two New Testaments and a Gospel of John. The books circulated so briskly that Tolya hardly had a chance to read them himself.

One of the prisoner-collaborators spotted the passing along of a New Testament and told his contact. The book was confiscated and the prisoner who had taken possession was put in solitary for a few days. Soon Tolya was summoned to appear before the camp authorities, who were furious. They accused him of having established a sect in the camp. This time he only received a warning, yet Tolya told the officer, 'You'd better remember that every person has to appear before God some day. You oppose God. If you do not repent, things will not go well with you.'

The first year Tolya had to do strenuous labour in a munitions factory, making hinges for munition cases. If he didn't deliver three thousand six hundred hinges each day, his food rations were cut or he was put in solitary. The target was impossible, even for powerful Tolya. Moreover, the authorities kept causing dissension between the prisoners so as to interrupt production. But within a year Tolya had many friends who protected him from the authorities. They also formed small sharing groups, outside and inside working hours, for they all wanted to hear what Tolya had to say about faith. One of the foremen — himself a prisoner — halved Tolya's target to free him for mission work. Prisoners, and even some officers, wanted to hear him.

One prisoner, a Muslim from Chichin, north of the Kaukasian mountains, showed as little fear as Tolya did. They often talked together and Tolya gave him a New Testament. At first the man kept saying, 'Allah is God and Mohammed is his prophet. Jesus cannot be the Son of God.' After having read the Word of God, he came to Tolya and said, 'There is no God but Allah, but Mohammed is not his prophet. Only the Son of God, Jesus Christ, is the great prophet and God is all in all.'

As his own Bible was continually read by others, Tolya worked to get another Bible for this Muslim friend. It took a lot of effort and money, but the gratitude of this brave Muslim prisoner was well worth it.

After eighteen months the Muslim was transferred to one of the most brutal gaols in the Soviet Union as a result of his contacts with Tolya. The camp authorities said that he had become an uneducable anti-communist.

As they couldn't discourage Tolya, either by solitary confinement or diminished food rations, the KGB thought up a punishment that was the equivalent of death. They transferred him to the terminal ward of the special camp hospital. Every morning he and the other eighty patients had to stand beside their beds, while guards tore the beds apart to look for contraband goods. Everybody who didn't get up had died during the night, but it sometimes took a few hours before the body was removed.

The stench was unbearable, and many TB patients constantly coughed up blood. Though suffering from a vitamin deficiency like most prisoners, Tolya was not really ill, but he remained under constant guard and had to stay in bed most of the time.

At first Tolya asked himself why he had been moved to this ward with all its risks. He had to overcome great reluctance to sit close to especially contagious patients. But as he managed to get to know some people, he understood that God had planned to use him here, to tell dying patients about Him.

A terminal TB patient was so grateful for Tolya's encouraging words that he offered him a cup of tomato juice. In this setting it would be an insult to refuse this generous gift, but Tolya knew how dangerous to his own health it would be to drink from that man's cup. But the last few words of the Gospel of Mark flashed through his head, and he prayed, 'Lord, You have promised that those who drink poison shall not die. I pray that You work this miracle as I drink this cup.' Then he put his mind to something else, drank the red juice as fast as he could, and then thanked the patient. God heard his prayer.

For as long as Tolya was on that ward the congregation in Chuguyevka prayed for him with great intensity. God had revealed to them that Tolya was surrounded by deadly viruses, but he remained protected against infection as though within a glass jar.

Nikolai Vins was prisoner in the labour camp Dzhanga, close to Krasnovodsk on the Caspian Sea. The fact that this so-called 'black camp' was run by criminals did not imply that the 'reds' had no influence here. The Communists kept a close watch on this prisoner. He too had made it clear, right away, that he would ignore the prohibition against talking about his faith, and it stirred the camp authorities to great anger. Together with the KGB they thought up all kinds of ways to make Nikolai's life miserable. But Nikolai too gained favour from ordinary prisoners and supervisors, and he even had positive contacts with some members of the military guard.

At first they made Nikolai manufacture steel gates, but when his body collapsed under the heavy work, his 'black' foreman gave him an easier job. As soon as the KGB noticed the transfer, they ripped his bed apart, and of course found a poem and a few scribbles about Nikolai's faith. They promptly threw him in a cell measuring two by two yards, in which seven other prisoners were already panting for air in a temperature of 45.50 degrees.

After ten days they took Nikolai to a quarry where he and about thirty other prisoners had to move heavy boulders in a wheelbarrow. He had been weakened severely and couldn't keep up the work. After a few hours he had reached the end of his tether. He cried out to God, 'Lord, I know You have placed me here for Your purpose, but if I need to do this, I pray You provide sufficient strength.' Before he even finished his prayer, the foreman asked him to operate the stone cutter. But when the supervisor saw that Nikolai had received easier work, he reproached the foreman, a Muslim prisoner. The foreman gave as good as he got, and Nikolai heard him yell, 'I need Vins, for he's the only one who can fix the bulldozer, which hasn't run for days.' And with a smile he turned to Nikolai and whispered, 'You can do that, can't you?' 'I'll try', Vins said to him, not feeling all that sure of himself. But after a few days of taking apart and putting together the bulldozer started, and Nikolai was even assigned to run it for a month. But then the KGB noticed his 'promotion', and made sure he was again 'demoted' immediately to something else.

Most of the prisoners there were Muslim nationalists, who had respect for Nikolai's public witness and belief. For them the most important criteria for other people included not being a Russian, and believing in God. They hated atheists and were always on the lookout for ways to obstruct them, often using hunger and labour strikes.

Most of the soldiers who guarded the camp were also non-Russian, in an attempt to prevent ethnic clashes. Nikolai got to know two Moldavians who had been brought up as Christians, cousins who had since left the faith. After many discussions, they asked for Nikolai's New Testament.

Two Ukrainian soldiers also expressed interest. One night one of them drank too much and 'borrowed' his officer's car, which he damaged in a collision. The next day he approached Nikolai, utterly distressed about having to go to court for his joy riding. 'May I borrow your Bible, I want to read it now.' Nikolai sensed the great need of this young fellow, but realized also that he would probably never see his New Testament again. 'What do you want to read it for? You don't even believe what it says', he said. But the boy persisted. 'Honest, I'll give it back to you.' Reluctantly Nikolai handed him his most precious possession. The next day he heard that the soldier had been transferred to Askhabad, and he regretted his generosity.

But after three days the joy rider returned it, looking chipper. 'Here's your book; it saved my life!' Nikolai was astonished. The soldier related the events in court. 'I put it in my inside pocket, over my heart. When I entered court, I put my hand on it and said, 'God, I pray for your blessing'. You won't believe it, but I haven't been discharged and I received no prison sentence. All I've got to do is pay for the damages. The God of the Bible has done that for me.' After this story Nikolai said, 'Go back to your bunk and kneel down. Bring your thanks to God and believe in Him.' The young officer replied, 'I already believe, for I know that this was surely a miracle from God.' After this they often talked together, even though Nikolai was never sure that the soldier had indeed made a genuine decision to believe in God.

Peter Walter became a prisoner in the area of

Krashnoyarks, north of the Mongolian border. For the first month he worked in a sawmill, but then he got an easier job in another camp. Every day the KGB summoned him, and every day they told him he would receive severe punishment if he didn't abandon his Christian faith. Not a day went by without this intimidation, sometimes as many as five times a day.

When it became clear that he wouldn't be persuaded by anyone, they brought him back to the much heavier work in the sawmill. There, prisoners had to work so hard that many landed up in the sick bay, more dead than alive. Fortunately, Peter was sustained by the food parcels from home, and neither hunger nor a shortage of vitamins made him ill.

The camp was surrounded by treacherous marshes, which prevented any direct approach by the Chuguyevka brothers. A sixty-year-old guard would meet them outside the marshes, bring the parcel in, bring a signed note back from Peter, and receive money for his services.

By the end of 1987, and as a result of Gorbachov's perestroika, the camp was closed and changed into an ordinary sawmill. But the prisoners were not released. Instead, they were transported to another camp, twenty miles away. For six months Peter was terrorized by an officer who carried a mortal hatred for the faith. Every day he was body-searched from top to toe, and threatened with severe punishment. Once the officer found a spiritual poem on a table in a barracks, and he placed Peter in solitary for fifteen days. The guards often woke Peter for interrogation, even in the middle of the night. But finally the KGB and the camp authorities gave up trying to persuade him to abandon his faith. They simply couldn't comprehend how a man as young as Peter could be so steadfast in his suffering for his God. The other prisoners, however, became convinced that Peter's faith had to be very special, seeing how much he valued it. Through many conversations, a number of prisoners came close to a choice for Jesus. Yet that step in this camp was so difficult that they preferred to say, 'As soon as I'm free again, I'll go to church.'

21
Visiting the Prisoners

The future of the ten prisoners rested in God's hands, but that was no reason simply to endure whatever happened. The congregation sorrowed, and sorrowed deeply. The suffering of the prisoners and the tyranny of the authorities weighed down heavily on them. Only constancy in prayer and diligence in pursuing unity would prevent slackening off, and that also meant taking great risks in letting the prisoners know that they had not been forgotten.

In the autumn of 1985 Yegor Betcher set out to visit his brother-in-law Anatoli Khokha. No one had managed to contact him in the camp just south of Chuguyevka. His wife Elvira and their children had been refused, in spite of an official invitation. At the last moment the KGB told her that Anatoli had been denied visiting privileges because of bad behaviour.

Someone who had been with Anatoli in the labour camp had come to Chuguyevka, to bring greetings and to tell them that he knew a secret way to meet Anatoli during working hours. Elvira and the other women filled a parcel with nourishing food and some items of clothing. Yegor brought along a valuable ginseng root, saved up especially for the ultra-lean Khokha, for a few drops of ginseng sap would be good medicine against malnutrition and lack of vitamins.

Yegor knew every inch of the taiga and drove the ex-prisoner back on his motorcycle. The man looked a bit ill at ease when they all prayed before their departure on their trip south, almost a hundred and twenty-five miles over a deserted forest road. On the way the passenger kept talking about emigration and West Germany, as if Yegor knew anything about life there. Yegor let him talk and kept his attention on the sandy road. About halfway the man asked whether Yegor could slow down, for his back was hurting him.

As Yegor eased back the throttle, everything turned black before his eyes. When he came to, men he recognized as forest workers were bending over him. The motorcycle lay in the ditch and he saw his passenger with the parcel meant for Anatoli under his arm. He was unhurt and mentioned something about an accident. Yegor had a splitting headache and lost consciousness again. Later he could only remember vaguely that he was put into the small bus of the forest workers.

When he regained consciousness he found himself in a hospital bed. A nurse told him that forest workers had found him and brought him to Sergeyevka. Only then did he remember that he had been on his way to Anatoli. 'What happened?' he asked the nurse. She said, 'Something heavy hit your head.' That same moment a policeman entered, rudely interrupting the nurse and motioning her to go away. He asked Yegor, 'Did you know your passenger?' 'I don't remember', said Yegor. 'Excellent', the officer said, and walked away without any more questions. A bit later a KGB agent asked Yegor the same question. When Yegor repeated that he couldn't remember and that he didn't know the man in any case, the KGB man said, 'Terrific'.

A nurse transferred him to another room in the middle of the night. She wanted to give him an injection, but somehow she couldn't penetrate Yegor's skin. She transferred the contents to another syringe, but that needle wouldn't work either. Yegor noticed that she was searching for the main artery, but his skin seemed like leather. She tried a few more times but couldn't do it. The nurse first cursed and raged, and then walked angrily away. After a few hours she returned, picked up the syringe and stuck the needle straight into the muscles of Yegor's upper arm, without any further trouble. Yegor was still too dopey from his accident to understand what was going on, but he did feel the shooting pain in his arm. The next morning he noticed that his arm was swollen and dark blue, from elbow to shoulder.

A bit later he heard a familiar voice he couldn't identify precisely, a man checking with the nurse. A doctor? The hospital director? They walked along the hall past the open door, and Yegor saw a familiar figure: the 'ex-prisoner', now in an expensive suit, was addressing the nurse who had given him the injection.

Suddenly he understood. The visit to Anatoli had been a pretext for getting rid of him, but God had saved him. He remembered that the man had asked him to slow down, probably to hit him with a steel object. Perhaps the uneven road had made it too difficult to hit him in the right spot.

Furthermore, the KGB agent had not counted on forest workers arriving at that moment in their little bus, and he had lied to them about an accident. The forest workers had brought Yegor into this hospital, where even the planned injection had gone awry. The whole setup had been an utter failure, and that would probably cost the KGB man his career. Now Yegor understood why the man had reacted so angrily.

He called out to the nurse for the name of the man. She looked frightened and asked Yegor, 'Don't you really know who that is?' Yegor answered, 'No, but I do know what he's planning to achieve. Why did you give me a needle last night?' He pointed to his upper arm and looked intently at the nurse. 'Me? I didn't give you a needle.' She ran away.

When Yegor didn't return the next day, his wife and the other Christians became worried. Vladimir Walter and

Valeri Lobsov began a search with another motorcycle. At one point they saw children playing motocross on Yegor's bike. The children told them that their fathers were forest workers, and that the previous owner had been taken to the hospital with an injury. Vladimir and Valeri quickly returned to Chuguyevka, suspecting yet one more KGB trick, for Yegor would not drive recklessly on a lonely forest road. They also saw that the bike had hardly been damaged.

Back in Chuguyevka they took a car for a trip to the Sergeyevka hospital, where they found Yegor with a thick bandage around his head and a revolting bulge on his upper arm. He told them what had happened, and against all protests by the doctors the two brothers took Yegor back to Chuguyevka.

Anatoli Khokha wasn't visited this time either, and if God had not prevented it, Yegor Betcher would have become yet one more victim of KGB medical care.

Some time later Yegor accidentally discovered the identity of the man, who, as it turned out, lived in Chuguyevka. Yegor recognized the bottle with the ginseng root that he had intended for Anatoli. There was no doubt about it, for ginseng roots all have their unique shape, and nature lover Yegor would never mistake one for another.

This incident led to the decision never to travel alone. When the prisoners' whereabouts became known two brothers were sent on visiting enterprises, which required steel nerves and especially great stamina. It became clear that Viktor Pavlovets was meant to serve as a deterrent for the rest of the congregation. He was a prisoner in a camp only four miles from Chuguyevka, but the camp was located in a wide open space and thus hard to approach without being spotted. Of course the Christians did everything they could to make contact with Viktor. Close to the camp they rented a small plot on which they cultivated potatoes and vegetables, hoping to gain a glimpse of him. Friedrich

Rosher and Valeri Pavolvets, Viktor's brother, had scouted the whole area and managed periodically to throw parcels over the fence. The goods reached Viktor most of the time because the other prisoners liked him. However, the prison authorities were furious at their inability to prevent this, especially because the parcels had to be thrown over five high walls topped with barbed wire. Once, a guard got hold of a parcel which had landed between the fourth and fifth walls. Of course the parcel had no name on it, but the guards knew that only one prisoner had such faithful friends outside. In the end they locked Viktor up in solitary for a period of three months.

By the end of 1985 the congregation knew the whereabouts of all but one of the prisoners. The only one missing was Viktor Samsonov. It took a full year before his location became known. The authorities had concentrated their efforts on the youngest of the members, attempting to persuade him to abandon his faith. When they hadn't succeeded even after a year, they gave him a job on the outside of the camp, in the town where his parents still lived. All the prisoners there were visited regularly, at least in the form of a food parcel via other prisoners or guards. Personal contact was almost impossible, and permission for official visits by family members was a rarity. More than once permission was arbitrarily denied after visitors had travelled for thousands of miles. Then, to prevent any possible glimpse of the prisoner, the guards would place him in isolation.

Nikolai Vins had two visits by his father-in-law in the thirty months that he stayed in the Dzhanga labour camp. Unfortunately this relative from Leninabad knew little of the condition of Olga and the children, or the Chuguyevka congregation. When he arrived for a third visit, he was told that Nikolai had been locked up in solitary because of 'anti-social behaviour'.

During that same period the Chuguyevka brothers managed to reach the camp only twice, but they did not manage to reach Vins over the fence. Nevertheless, the attempts had important consequences, for all the other prisoners were deeply impressed by the fact that Nikolai had such devoted friends, who would travel such a distance without official travel permits, braving even the heavily-guarded border with Iran. Nikolai, as well as the other prisoners, was greatly encouraged by this obvious token of love.

During the daytime a prisoner would sit 'on guard' on the roof of a construction shed near the camp fence, from where he could observe the long straight road into the camp. Of course the soldiers in the watchtowers had the same view, and it wasn't easy to approach the camp unobserved. Nevertheless, occasionally attempts were successful, and then not much time was left to make contact. This was the reason for the prisoner's 'watch'.

One day, the 'guard' didn't know how, two men stood on the road, calling out, 'Hey, do you know Nikolai?' 'Which one?' said the prisoner. 'Nikolai from the Vladivostok prison! We'll be back in thirty minutes. Make sure he's in your spot.'

Vladimir Walter and Johan Vins had made the long journey mostly by plane. They had been subject to frequent inspections, but God had provided crucial miracles of diversion when they had to show their travel permits. The scrap paper Vladimir had with him didn't even look like one from a distance, but the police never seemed to notice the difference.

And so now they stood in front of the high wall which separated them from the prisoners. No one had heard or seen them, except this prisoner lookout. While waiting in a shady spot, they hoped he wasn't a stool-pigeon.

After thirty minutes they rose and immediately spotted

Nikolai. Words could not describe their emotions and joy. Alas, they had no wings to fly over the fence and embrace each other. After Nikolai had gained control of his emotions again, he called out, 'We'll have no more than ten minutes. I've got five fellows standing lookout.'

The distance between them was about six yards, with two walls of two and a half yards in between. 'What do you think,' Vladimir said, 'could we throw a parcel across?' Nikolai didn't realize how heavy the food parcel would be and called out, 'I think so, but take care that it doesn't fall in between, for then I'm in trouble.' Johan took a run at it before he threw the parcel with all his might, but to his consternation it proved too heavy and fell in between the two high walls. 'Quick,' Johan told Vladimir, 'help me up the wall.' They had no time to weigh up the risks and Vladimir boosted him up. Johan found himself between the two walls and attempted to throw the parcel over the inner one, but still couldn't do it. From his high vantage point Nikolai saw how closely Johan brushed past the alarm wires to try again, and called out, 'Johan, divide it up into two parcels'. Johan did, and this time managed to toss everything inside the camp.

Nikolai's fellow prisoner lookouts quickly ran to the stuff and distributed the items in order to hide them. They all knew the camp's golden rule: move contraband away from your immediate presence, and preferably remain ignorant of its location. If you need anything, ask the person who hid it for you, and compensate him for it. The prisoner who violated this rule could expect severe sanctions.

The two brothers looked intently at each other for the last time. Words failed them. 'Quick,' Nikolai said, 'go back!' Johan's eyes were full of tears and he replied, 'Hold fast, brother', before he climbed back over the outer wall. Vladimir had been waiting, hearing or seeing nothing, and had become worried. 'Maybe Johan has injured himself', he thought, but the moment he decided to climb onto the wall to find out, Johan's head appeared. Even before his feet reached the ground, bedlam broke loose. Johan had probably touched a warning wire, for from one of the watch towers a signal was given, and within seconds all kinds of sirens were going.

Vladimir and Johan ran away as fast as they could. Behind some bushes they dropped to the ground, panting. They spotted soldiers inspecting the walls, but there were no signs that they would be followed.

Without mishap they reached the Krasnovodosk airport. Normally, travel by air was far too expensive for the Chuguyevka Christians, but because he was now the congregation's pastor, Vladimir couldn't stay away too long. When they reached Vladivostok airport, the plane halted in the middle of the tarmac, where it stayed for a long time before a loudspeaker announced: 'We regret to inform you that on police orders no one may leave the plane before inspection of all travel permits. Please prepare them for inspection.'

The two couriers realized that this inspection was connected with their visit. They sat in seats with the aisle in between, and when the officer approached them they offered their invalid papers. The man looked at them closely . . . and returned them without saying a word. The two travellers had a hard time hiding their relief. When they reached home a police inspector arrived to inquire where they had been, but neither one answered, and the inspector had almost nothing to go on to arrest them.

The road of the Chuguyevka congregation was like an expedition to the Himalayas. They travelled as on a narrow mountain path, where the slightest wrong step could be fatal. There was no going back, and every step ahead was fraught with danger. They had blindly to trust their Guide, Who, of course, was nothing but the Best there could be!

Now entirely without human support and security, they walked closely behind Him. As in the days of the disciples, they were eye-witnesses to many miracles. Healing was as common as in earlier days, when they went to doctors, except that now everyone was healed. But the most miraculous events surrounded the visits to the prisoner brothers.

If you don't really believe in the communion of saints, you will not be willing to sacrifice much for it. Then you would call 'reckless' a trip made by hanging on to the ice-covered steel bars of a railway oil truck because travelling in a passenger train is too risky. But Friedrich Rosher, already minus one hand because of an earlier accident, thought the risk necessary while on his way to his brother in prison! That brother could not be allowed to forget that he too belonged to the Church. Of course the food parcel was important too, but more important than that was the gesture, the enormous love of which the parcel spoke: the long and dangerous journey, the standing patiently before a closed set of gates, the risk of throwing the parcel over a wall, or giving it to a guard who might or might not be trustworthy, about the iron will needed to keep going on behalf of someone else.

Why did Friedrich Rosher have to hang on to a railway tanker with one hand? Why did Vladimir Walter arrive in Khabarovsk covered in black coal dust, the result of travelling in the engine's tender? Why did Yegor Betcher and Gennadi Maydanyuk crawl through mud and snow for hundreds of yards, so that they could get out of Chuguyevka?

The reasons were clear: the Primorski KGB was hunting a small group of Chuguyevka Christians. Before these Christians had arrived, this province had already been a territory full of military barracks, air bases, border posts and secret installations. But now the KGB added reinforcements to the standard guard posts, and they added a number of other posts as well.

In earlier days each train between Vladivostok and Khabarovsk might have been inspected once or twice, but now it was known that Christians might be on the road to visit their fellow believers, a thorough inspection was carried out at each station stop. Trained dogs sniffed the outside, while a small army of trained soldiers combed the inside of the train.

A friendly Christian from another congregation told them that he once sat across from two officers who were discussing these severe measures. He heard one say to the other, that the measures were directed against a group of Christians who lived somewhere in Primorski and who travelled without proper permits. The officer expressed his indignation that these people ignored the laws of the Soviet Union and caused so much delay.

Once Yegor Betcher and Wilhelm Rosher took a scheduled passenger train on the heavily protected Vladivostok-Khabarovsk line, at midnight, when an intense inspection was unlikely. They arrived in Dalnerechensk at 2 a.m. All lights went on on the platform, and the dogs began their usual job, but when the two passengers saw the uncommonly large number of military, they knew that the KGB was on their trail, and they showed their 'papers' as requested. But this time something went wrong.

Wilhelm and Yegor were transported to an army camp, thirty miles to the south. Halfway there the Black Raven broke down, and the soldiers left them locked up in the bitter cold while they went for a replacement. Towards the morning they continued their trip to a former Japanese bunker, where for eighteen days they sat in a dark, damp cell. Its walls and ceiling were studded with concrete knobs that made it impossible to sit against the wall or stand up straight. The smell was atrocious, and it became worse after their daily meal of fish guts.

When they returned home after the eighteen days, completely exhausted and starving, it was clear that they could only travel through Primorski via the safer routes through the taiga or by means of freight trains, until God showed them other options.

22
In and Out of Moscow

After a long absence, education inspector Viktor Romanov showed up again. Long ago the campaign of slander against the Chuguyevka Christians had primarily targeted the children. Romanov had announced: 'All Soviet children are state property. If you insist on having "our" children at your worship services, we'll bring them up. We have received Moscow's permission to remove them if you continue to torture them spiritually.'

By now thirty-one of those "poor" children were deprived of the presence of their fathers, and seventy-five children between the ages of four and sixteen couldn't go to school. Yet Romanov's most serious threat had not yet been executed. The children were still at home, assisting in the many chores designed to help the community survive, and taking an occasional stab at the school books they had around.

Romanov appeared to have made a one-hundred-and-eighty degree turn. Politely greeting Anna and Vladimir Walter, he requested permission to enter their home. 'You understand I'm here because of the children', he began. Vladimir nodded and waited. 'How are they doing? They've not been to school for many months. Can I be of any help?' Vladimir was astonished at this solicitude and told him that the children would occasionally glance inside the school books, but with the problems of the last few months they hadn't been able to study regularly.

As always when a member of the authorities came to visit

any member, a number of other fathers and mothers soon arrived. Everyone was astonished when the inspector continued, 'Mr Walter, it is my responsibility to see to it that all Chuguyevka children receive a good education, so I propose that you pick up the books you need from the school and design a timetable for each age group.'

Aha! A sign that dissension might exist in high places about ways to deal with them? After Romanov left, they all went on their knees to praise God. It wasn't that they were convinced that this experienced atheist had changed his own mind, for it was clear he had been delegated to bring this message, perhaps even by the KGB. But here was at least a first step forward on the road to the victory God had promised them.

Vladimir visited the school where the children had received so much abuse. The principal hadn't been informed yet and responded with his usual arrogance: 'Absolutely not, why should I help you?' He telephoned the inspector and promptly walked out of his office, clearly irritated. When he returned he barked, 'The custodian downstairs has your books. You may go.'

During that first year, when the ten were still prisoners, it proved difficult to design a curriculum. Only after Gennadi Maydanyuk and Anatoli Khokha had been released by late February 1986, were serious attempts made to set up a private school. Gennadi organized some groupings for the children, and involved mothers, grandmothers and older children in teaching. Mariya Walter and Lyudmila Teplikh took grade one, and Olga Sheludkova grade two. Above that, a specific 'teacher' was assigned for each subject, and that included grandfathers and grandmothers, who tutored children and supervised homework.

Real classrooms were established in some of the houses, where the children received five hours of instruction in an atmosphere of sound discipline. The babies of 'teacher' mothers were looked after by other mothers. The school turned into a blessing for the whole community. Everyone was involved and the studies diverted the attention of the children from all the traumatic experiences of the past months.

Of course each day began with religious instruction, a good opportunity to pray together and meditate on God's plan as revealed in the Bible. This private school in Chuguyevka was the first and for a time the only Soviet school that featured religious instruction!

But soon the parents realized that they couldn't go on in this way. Their children needed a regular education as well as a life free from street harassment. Of course, some people in Chuguyevka now looked upon them with favour, but you never knew who had been stirred up against them by the KGB. Viktor Romanov's sudden transformation was linked to Moscow's surprise about the tenacity with which these Christians had defended their rights. Atheists had been brought up expecting Christians to sit in dark corners awaiting their eternal life, but the actions of these Chuguyevka Christians had upset their stereotyped view. These Christians let themselves be arrested without resistance on the one hand, but on the other they boldly, and without regard for their personal safety, challenged the monopoly of the communist government.

During and after the 1985 trials congregational priorities had changed dramatically. Mission work remained important, but almost equally important was the continued care for their imprisoned brothers. They also needed to concern themselves with their own survival as a group. God had promised them deliverance from this misery, but how deliverance would come about no one knew. Long ago they had decided to leave Central Asia for this mission field, but now their children's future was in jeopardy. Here they couldn't receive a sound education or training in a trade. Romanov's threats had manoeuvred them into expressing a desire to emigrate. And this one thing the Chuguyevka Christians had learned quickly: if you plan to confront the KGB, don't waver; never give them an opportunity to make decisions for you, but stay on your own course.

'You're so young still and you don't realize whom you have challenged', said an old pentecostal who had spent twenty-one of his own years in labour camps because of his faith. He visited them for the sole purpose of warning them against the tremendous power of the KGB. The elders then asked him, 'What must we do? Advise us. You're experienced and an authoritative spiritual leader. Tell us.' 'Disperse in smaller groups', the man said. 'Don't form such a cohesive target, for your unity is what makes them so angry.' The young elders looked at each other and understood that fear drove this prominent Christian. He offered the same counsel that had caused so much grief in the past by isolating Christians from each other.

The discussion confirmed their own stance even more, and no one was left with any doubt: all decisions had to be communally made. The KGB needed to know that these Christians were united and determined to reach their goal. Perhaps this conviction was the most important reason why they persisted with their emigration plans. Moreover, they knew that Soviet leaders were becoming more sensitive to pressure from abroad.

For the second Chuguyevka trial, at the end of April 1985, Leonard Voitke and Wilhelm Rosher travelled to Moscow in utter secrecy. The KGB did not expect anyone to make such a trip, especially during that week, and that's why the travellers reached the capital without any interference. Their plan had already taken some shape in Chuguyevka, but they were charged with making it work here. First they walked past the German embassy a few times, where one policeman stood on guard while several others walked around the complex. During the day the gate appeared to be unlocked and easy to open quickly. They decided simply to enter. In the eventuality that they would be stopped, they also formulated an alternative plan.

The next day Wilhelm and Leonard walked up to the gate. The burly policeman demonstratively stepped forward to intercept them. Leonard showed him an official document that contained an invitation to enter West Germany. As nonchalantly as he could manage, he said, 'I need a small alteration to it, please let me pass'. The policeman eyed the document suspiciously and then challenged him in the way of a schoolyard bully: 'Show me your passport first.' It was the moment for the alternative plan. While Leonard handed him his identity card, Wilhelm quickly ran towards the embassy's front door, some fifteen yards from the guard house. The policeman ran after him, but he was too late.

Wilhelm stood inside, on German soil. Here he was safe, but he felt miserable thinking of Leonard who would be in deep trouble, he was sure. But they carefully rehearsed the scenario, minute by minute. Because Wilhelm spoke better German, he was the logical person to speak to the Ambassador.

While Wilhelm stood catching his breath, a nattily dressed gentleman approached him. 'Are you the Ambassador?' the intruder asked. The man replied in clipped and perfect German, 'No, I'm the Consul. Who are you and what can I do for you?'

Wilhelm told him his story. He handed the man a bundle of documents he had carefully carried in his inside pocket, and told them of the suffering of this congregation of former Germans, and their problems in educating their children. He also told them that his close friend had probably been arrested outside the gate a moment ago.

The man carefully listened to the story, but took no initiative. Without showing any feeling, he said, 'I'm sorry, but I can't be of service. The Ambassador is in Geneva at the moment in connection with the summit meeting between Gorbachov and Reagan.' He then entered a room and let Wilhelm wait a full fifteen minutes. From a word here and there Wilhelm concluded that he was discussing the matter by telephone with some superiors. When the man returned, he nodded and said, 'I have to disappoint you'.

Wilhelm felt defeated. Was this the representative of the same country his father, grandfather and great-grandfather had been proud of? With his voice cracking, he said, 'Sir, don't you realize that seven members of our congregation, including my own blood brother Bernhard, stand before a judge merely because they want to exercise freedom of religion? They want to emigrate because they still feel themselves more German than Russian.'

After two hours of fruitless conversation the Consul took Wilhelm's arm to guide him outside through the open front door.

'Sorry,' he said once more, 'I can't do a thing for you', and he sounded as if he had rehearsed the phrase. Once outside, Wilhelm was roughly grabbed by two policemen and dragged along the path past the man who had first tried to stop him. 'I'll beat you to a pulp', that one yelled angrily, while trying to push his two colleagues away. 'I'll teach you a lesson that will turn you meek as a lamb and you won't dare leave Primorski ever again.' A KGB officer intervened and told him to shut up and go back to his post.

Wilhelm was placed on the back seat of a black Volga between two guards and taken to police quarters, where he met Leonard Voitke, already badly bruised. Both of them were interrogated for a long time. The KGB pretended not to know anything about their problems, feigning great surprise when they heard about the Chuguyevka trials and the KGB misdeeds there.

'Boy, oh boy, that just can't be true. Our organization doesn't do things like that. We only help people.' In the end the two Chuguyevka Christians were released on their promise that they would immediately return to their homes.

On their way back to the airport they were followed, but they managed to lose their shadows by suddenly jumping on a moving bus. When they arrived back in Primorski, the KGB of course already knew of their Moscow incident. They were waiting for the travellers, but God blinded their eyes when the brothers arrived back in Vladivostok, each on a separate flight on consecutive days. On 1st May they arrived safely back home, two days after the 'guilty' verdicts on their brothers.

That same evening new plans were drawn up. Even Leonard Voitke, badly abused as he was, stood squarely behind the plan to repeat the attempt, but now at the American embassy. They decided not to fly but to take the train, and with a team of four for greater safety: Leonard Voitke, Wilhelm Rosher, Benjamin Samsonov and Johan Vins. They left on the night of 2nd–3rd May, travelling through the taiga by car, to the far edge of Primorski. They crawled through barbed wire barriers and reached Dalnerechensk, where they knew an old Christian. Because the man had been converted while a criminal in gaol, he wasn't afraid of much and was always prepared to host the brothers. When they knocked on his door in the middle of the night, he quickly let them in and supplied food, and hot water for a welcome wash. After a few hours' rest they took the train to Khabarovsk, with tickets their friend had already purchased so that they didn't have to stand in the open on the platform. Only after all inspectors and soldiers had left the train did they board it from the rear.

After six days and nights of train travel they arrived in

Moscow, on 9th May, the day on which the Soviet Union celebrates liberation from the Nazis. The American embassy was closed, but they had good friends in the city with whom they could stay. The next day they cased the complex, and found that this embassy was protected even more closely than the German one. They took their time observing the movements of the guards, and only on 13th May did they put their plan into action, just after lunch.

They needed all four of them, for the plan was tricky. They knew they wouldn't get permission to enter, and storming the place would be impossible, what with two additional guards in front of the embassy door. They needed to be quick, and they had rehearsed their plan carefully. Yet they encountered more problems than they had foreseen.

Wilhelm Rosher tells the story:

'Even before we reached the gate we heard shouts: "Present your passports", as if they knew we were coming, and perhaps they did know because we had escaped our earlier pursuers. They had their guard up and wasted no time. Benjamin Samsonov let himself be grabbed at the gate, while Johan, Leonard and I ran to the door where the two other guards stood waiting. Behind us we heard yelling and the sound of a heavy beating. Benjamin was getting it in the teeth.

'At the door they first grabbed Leonard. We had noticed that the door opened outwards, not inwards; that's why someone had to be a sacrificial lamb to clear a path for the other. That was my job, and Johan spotted the opening between the guard and the doorpost, and quickly scooted inside. That same moment someone yanked my hair. My feet were already inside and my hands held the door tight, but the other guards grabbed my feet and tore me loose. The first clung to my hair, the second grabbed my arms and the third yanked my collar so hard that I almost choked.

They dragged me through the garden to an office around the corner from the embassy building. Leonard was already on the floor being brutally kicked and beaten by a burly policeman. I was thrown next to him, and three or four men kicked and beat us until the linoleum was red with our blood. Then the door opened and a heavy man entered, in a suit, but obviously a KGB official. He looked like a gentleman, but when he opened his mouth that image disappeared quickly. "Why didn't you shoot these bastards immediately?! You've let one escape and the other is now sipping tea with the Ambassador!"

'After a long time we were permitted to rise. We wiped the blood off our faces while they pushed us outside. They herded us like cattle to a waiting car, a black Volga with yellowing curtains across the back window. To stop eye contact with a number of foreign correspondents who stood outside the gate, our heads were pushed down on our shoes during the trip to the KGB office. After a wild race through the city we reached our destination and we were locked up in a cell.'

Back at the American embassy, Johan Vins was in conversation with a man whose specific responsibility it was to monitor human rights. He listened with a great deal of sympathetic attention and compassion. Johan concluded that he would try to do something, but unfortunately the Ambassador was in Geneva. However, he promised that he would telephone that day to inform his superior of the events in Moscow and Chuguyevka.

Johan wanted to stay inside the embassy, but the official persuaded him not to. Through a back gate, an American embassy car drove him deep into the city. But this kind of car is conspicuous in a city full of Volgas and Ladas, and when Johan got out at a subway entrance, two men quickly grabbed him. They took him to the same place where his two friends were already locked up.

Benjamin Samsonov was the only one still at large. He had managed to free himself from the grip of the policeman at the gate. The moment he knew Johan was inside the embassy, his own mission was completed. He had received a deep cut in his lip and was bleeding from several other places. He made his way to his lodging address, where he hid for a few days until his wounds had healed.

The other three were thoroughly investigated. The KGB threatened to charge them, but after a few days the threats softened. The embassy man had indeed acted. Via Western media and especially Voice of America radio broadcasts, the Chuguyevka situation was now world news. Items about it could be heard almost every day, even in Chuguyevka itself. The American ambassador in Geneva had officially asked his Russian counterpart for an explanation.

After three days the three men were released. Followed closely by KGB agents, they departed for the train station. Ignoring a long queue, a KGB agent guided them to a ticket office, telling others that they would miss the train otherwise. In their compartment, a *provodnik* (train steward) received instructions that had the effect of making wagon number six a prison for six days and seven nights. A KGB agent made the rounds to tell the other passengers that they were three dangerous criminals, and to avoid all contact. At each station the *provodnik* informed a local KGB man about their behaviour. About sixty miles before Chuguyevka, the Primorski head of the KGB personally took them off the train and drove them to their own front doors.

Two days later Benjamin Samsonov also arrived home.

23
Ora et Labora

Some Chuguyevka people, notably close neighbours, thought it scandalous that these peaceful people were persecuted so cruelly, especially because the Christians were always prepared to help others. These good people would call the Christian children inside to give them treats. A widow who lived in the same street as Vladimir Walter, often handed out tins of milk powder and other foods that would keep, meant for the prisoners. She remembered how the Christians had helped her when her husband was ill, and she was glad now to do something in return.

The deep conviction of the Chuguyevka Christians that their suffering would be only temporary and that God would liberate them soon, gave them unimaginable resilience. KGB collaborators continued to harass them. They wept sometimes, it is true, but always in secret, for God had revealed to them not to show their tears to their enemies. Miraculously, they didn't find that overly hard to do.

During one of many winter evenings when they were together they heard a noise at the window. Two brothers went out to look and saw footsteps in the snow from window to street. A few days later, a KGB officer said, 'How come you always laugh and sing, even with your problems?' One of them answered, 'We are convinced that God is stronger than all of your organization together. So it was you who spied on us through our window, two nights ago at nine o'clock?' The man felt sheepish and gave no reply.

It slowly began to dawn on the authorities that these Christians would never be prepared to relinquish their trust in God. Enduring everything, they remained positive and cheerful, paid no attention to barriers in their way, and managed even to attract worldwide attention to themselves.

In the course of 1986 Moscow talk began to include *glasnost* and *perestroika*. Some internationally famous dissidents were released. Yet here in faraway Primorski, the provincial KGB elected to increase their tough, even life-threatening measures.

On the evening of Gennadi Maydanyuk's return from his labour camp term the haystack behind his house went up in flames. Gennadi was at Johan Vins's house for a sauna, and when he returned home he saw the flames high above the roof of his house. Severe frost and dry conditions allowed for only a few pails of water. Most of the cattle fodder needed for four more winter months, was lost. Insufficient feed would lead to lower milk production, and that with so many growing children dependent on milk.

The police didn't think that an investigation was necessary. 'Probably your own children did it, playing with matches', they said. Gennadi had heard enough lies over the past year. Indignantly he turned around and on his way to the door said, 'Perhaps my little eight-month Olga did. She likes to play close to the haystack in twenty-five degrees below freezing at night!' The next winter Valeri Lobsov's haystack suffered the same fate, and again police blamed the children. This time it happened at 4 a.m., while everybody was asleep.

As far as Mr Kumchenko was concerned – third secretary of the Primorski communist party – harassment could go on forever. 'We'll push you so hard that you'll come to beg us on your knees for a crust of bread.'

But God continued to provide for their needs. The deacons distributed whatever food there was equally among all. Money remained a problem, for no one had a regular income any more, and the revenues of their forest products were insufficient. Yet God continuously provided. Money arrived, sometimes without anyone knowing where it came from. A Christian from one of the sister congregations perhaps? A stranger from far away? But whenever anyone discovered such an anonymous gift in a drawer or a coat pocket, it was put into the communal treasury.

This unity and the many prayers enabled them to endure their suffering. As a whole the Chuguyevka congregation was less concerned with its own fate than with that of the prisoners, who each stood alone against the might of KGB, guards and criminals.

Viktor Pavlovets was frequently locked up in isolation. Oleg Lobanov could only be visited when the ice had melted, for his labour camp was located at the far tip of a peninsula in the Lyena river, close to the city of Lensk. Viktor Walter was always under KGB pressure. Tolya Sheludkov and Nikolai Vins had to work terribly hard. Viktor Samsonov and Bernhard Rosher were always under severe psychological pressure, and the KGB didn't let up in trying to persuade Peter Walter to abandon his faith.

The Christians knew that the KGB had only one objective: to break up the unity of the congregation at any cost. get the prisoners to abandon all hope, and persuade the community to give up the struggle. As a special campaign of support for the prisoners, the congregation organized a sixth hunger strike, between 10th and 25th April 1986. They cried out to God to make known to Him their sorrow, knowing that He knew the needs of each prisoner.

Of course the children didn't take part in the fast, but they did participate in daily prayers. They counted it a great blessing to know that at that same hour the prisoners would also offer secret prayers in their respective camps.

These hours of prayer were undoubtedly the most moving moments of each day. Young and old knelt down in each living room. The children would pray to their heavenly Father to protect their earthly fathers, and for blessings in the labour camp. They would also remember the two unmarried prisoners, Viktor Pavlovets and Viktor Samsonov. They prayed so simply, but with their whole heart!

And God heard their prayers, but not in a way that was always comprehensible to everyone. In fact it appeared that at first matters got much worse.

Viktor Pavlovets had lifted too heavy a load in the steel factory, and had to have a hernia operation, in a special prisoners' hospital in Vladivostok, where family and friends were not permitted. Here too the KGB tried to entice him into collaboration, but he told them they would have to kill him before he would turn into a Judas. Lieutenant-Colonel Bykov told him: 'Viktor, we now know you won't co-operate with us, but tell them the truth at least. Write and say that we'll punish you even more if they don't stop their hunger strike.'

As sick as he was, Viktor looked the KGB officer right in the eye and said, 'I'm only in danger if they stop fasting and praying. I won't write.' Bykov smirked at this dose of determination and asked, 'And if I promise you visitors? What about it then?' Viktor turned his head away and his short 'No!' indicated that the conversation had come to an end. 'OK, then we'll get you to another camp, where your friends won't be able to reach you at all.' And with those words Bykov departed.

After fifteen days Viktor had not improved. He felt even worse than before the operation, yet they did transfer him, back to the same camp close to Chuguyevka. Apparently Bykov had decided to keep him near, in view of the excellent collaboration between KGB and camp government. A number of guards told Viktor their personal assurance that they would break his faith.

Viktor spent a total of three hundred days in solitary. The camp authorities, assisted by about twenty prisoner collaborators, found pretext after pretext to punish him. For example: unnoticed a lieutenant slipped three roubles into Viktor's pocket, and then called for some guards to frisk him, smirking when they found the money. The result: fifteen more days in solitary for Viktor.

Most of his punishment was the result of stool-pigeons reporting his contacts with other prisoners. For instance, Viktor got ten days for talking to a Jehovah's Witness who was also there because of his faith.

But most of the other prisoners loved it when Viktor talked to them about his faith, and that surprised the atheist camp authorities. They thought no one in Primorski would be interested in God. Major Grigori Gevashelishvili, in the course of a tirade, said, 'Viktor, shut your mouth about that God of yours. I'll tell you who is god here:it's me. In this camp I'm god.'

So, during 1986 it was almost impossible for the prisoners and the Chuguyevka Christians to find evidence that God was hearing their prayers. Yet they never wavered in expecting imminent change, nor in knowing that they did not stand alone in their struggles.

The West was beginning to learn about them, and there were indications that pressures were being exerted on the Kremlin. The first to notice was Viktor Walter, in the Matygori camp, near a little village close to Arkhangelsk. He had been transferred there from Velsk, for the KGB had concluded that he needed even heavier punishment in a camp three hundred miles farther north. On his arrival there, Captain Bibyayev, the camp commandant, had left him in no doubt about what would he could expect here. 'Do you know why they brought you here? Here we can show you what a real labour camp is like. Let's be clear: we'll pile accusation upon accusation, and you'll disappear into solitary; also we'll add years to your sentence. I've got orders to let you perish.'

Captain Bibyayev and his accomplices matched deeds with words, but God surrounded Viktor with prisoners who were on his side, who gained deep respect for this man who didn't compromise one inch in the same kind of protection from prisoner leaders as in Vladivostok prison.

From his Chuguyevka food parcels he arranged small caches in secret places. If he noticed another prisoner in critical physical shape, he shared his stocks. Sometimes he used them for a prisoner who had a birthday, but he discovered that the most appreciated present here was often a Western birthday card with a Bible verse printed on it. Through it all strong bonds developed between Viktor and the other prisoners, and he managed to speak freely to them about his faith.

But the most profound impression made was as a result of the attempted visits by his friends from far away. Viktor came to be seen as the most important prisoner in this camp, for no one else had such dedicated friends, and no one received as much foreign mail.

Yegor Betcher and Benjamin Samsonov arrived in Matygori by bus. This little village just south of Arkhangelsk was only inhabited by ex-prisoners, exiles and camp guards. Matygori was connected to the camp by a narrow country road, the only way in through a marshy area.

The two had made the trip in ten days, using planes and trains. Yegor used the passport of an unbelieving brother who also lived in Chuguyevka, while Benjamin used a passport of one of his brothers who lived in Soviet Central Asia. The trip had been uneventful thus far, but now they hit a snag. In the middle of the winter, darkness fell at

3 p.m., and they couldn't return to Arkhangelsk that day. They would be forced to stay in Matygori overnight.

They discovered that even in Chuguyevka the people were more hospitable than here. For hours they knocked on doors to ask for a night's lodging, but in vain. It seemed that no one cared whether they froze to death. Finally they came upon an old man who was chopping wood in his front yard, and who laboriously straightened himself when they accosted him. He looked sharply at the two frozen visitors and asked, 'Where are you from?' Yegor replied, 'From the province of Primorski, close to the Sea of Japan.' The old man placed his axe on the ground and said, 'That far? You must be here because of the camp. Go inside, it's warm there.'

The house was untidy and dirty, but they were cold and tired enough only to feel gratitude. The man remained standing at the stove and said, 'I thought, if you have come that far to visit a friend, you fellows must be all right.' While he boiled the kettle he told them: 'I was in there for eight years myself. Now I'm an exile here. They watch me all the time, but old Ivan isn't afraid of them any more.' He shuffled to a rickety chair and sat down. Once more he carefully observed his two shivering guests and said, 'People who care for those poor prisoners are less foolish than the folk who live around here. They don't care for anybody any more, they murder without blinking an eye. I take it that your friend isn't just an ordinary prisoner either.'

Suddenly the front door was thrown open, and a bunch of drunks tried to enter, immediately threatening the two guests. But the old man was surprisingly strong and pushed them back. He yelled at them: 'You're blind drunk and I have family visitors. Get out!'

'We didn't know you had family left, Ivan', they yelled back, while the old man firmly bolted his door.

In the morning Yegor and Benjamin started out early to find someone to get the food parcel to Viktor. The rough road to the camp turned out to be guarded heavily, with police officers everywhere. It almost seemed as if they had been tipped off. To make matters worse, a woman spotted them and reported that she had seen two suspicious characters. Yegor and Benjamin had to hide for a bit, until the danger lessened. After a while they decided to proceed through a stand of birch trees, where the snow reached to their knees and the marshy soil had not frozen over in spite of very low temperatures. With each step their boots sunk down deeper, and two or three times they found themselves in ice cold water up to their waists. Soon they were both soaked through and had hardly any feeling left in their limbs.

After an exhausting journey through the swamp, they finally reached the road to the camp. A horse and cart arrived at that precise moment, an opportunity they both felt they should make use of. When the cart was close enough, they came out of their hiding place. The driver was startled, and from deep inside his fur hat he eyed his 'raiders' with deep suspicion.

They tried to find out why he was going to the camp, and discovered that he was picking up potato peelings and other scraps, and that he had no other link to the guards. When they asked him to take a letter along, he grew scared. 'You realize I'll be gaoled if they catch me with it.' But after they promised him a substantial reward, he agreed. They only gave him a letter this time. The next day they would wait here for Viktor's reply.

After waiting for three hours in the bitter cold the next day, Viktor and Yegor saw him approaching, and he had Viktor's letter. Viktor wrote that they had hit upon the right man: 'Dear brothers, I'm so glad you have come. This man is reliable, and you can give him whatever you have.'

They handed the driver a small packet containing a Bible, tea, food and money, the second half of the reward they had promised him, and which Viktor would give him on arrival, after he had inspected the contents with the help of a list. They agreed to meet again two days later to pick up Viktor's letters and to give him the rest of the reward.

Yegor and Benjamin disappeared into the swamp again, trying to retrace their steps, but it was already dark and they soon could only see the white birch trunks. Within thirty minutes they were totally lost. They kept sinking deeply into the soft soil and sometimes stayed down in the snow, too discouraged to move. They continuously prayed to God to help them find their way back, but it seemed they were praying in vain. 'But we did accomplish our objective', Yegor told himself to gain a bit of courage. Finally they hit a hard patch of ground, a path which led to the road back to Matygori.

When they reached the house of Ivan, the old man saw how they had suffered and said, 'Take your wet clothes off and get under the blankets.' They followed his advice and crawled naked underneath all the blankets and coats Ivan had. The old man stirred up his woodstove and soon they both slept soundly.

Ivan bought an extra quantity of potatoes – a luxury in a polar area this far off the beaten track – but because he had 'family' visiting, no questions were asked. For as long as the two Chuguyevka brothers were with him, he kept others away. The two told him about their lives, their conversions, and about congregational life. Ivan was deeply impressed, for he hadn't ever heard anything like it. But with his own eyes he saw how these people supported each other. Over nine thousand miles to visit a friend! And not once, but repeatedly!

After this visit Ivan came to meet other brothers too, for some made as many as five trips to Matygori to supply their friend and pastor with news and essential food. Once some came for nothing, for the KGB had hermetically sealed off the whole area, having followed them all the way from Chuguyevka.

Old Ivan remained an exile for the moment, but he pledged that he would come to Chuguyevka immediately after his release.

24
Exodus: First a Trickle, then a Flood

Once during the weekly prayer meeting someone was moved to read 2 Corinthians 1:8–11. The hearers were struck by the similarity to their own circumstances.

'We do not want you to be uninformed, brothers, about the hardships we suffered in the province of Asia. We were under great pressure, far beyond our ability to endure, so that we despaired even of life. Indeed, in our hearts we felt the sentence of death. But this happened that we might not rely on ourselves but on God, who raises the dead. He has delivered us from such a deadly peril, and he will deliver us. On him we have set our hope that he will continue to deliver us, as you helped us by your prayers. Then many will give thanks on our behalf for the gracious favour granted us in answer to the prayers of many.'

The apostle Paul wrote these words in the past tense. He had already born the 'great pressure', and that knowledge gave the Chuguyevka Christians hope. They too would be delivered from their suffering.

But who would intercede on their behalf with prayers? They were so geographically isolated. True, they had sent photographs, films, letters and other documents to the West, and even the President of the United States knew of their circumstances. But were 'ordinary' folk praying for them also? One KGB officer had once told them, with a smirk on his face, 'How come politicians make a big fuss about you, while ordinary Christians remain silent?'

But was it true? Until 1987 their suffering was known

only to people who made it their profession to work on behalf of dissidents and those who were persecuted because of their faith. But more than that, a special campaign had been started already to pray for Christians in the Soviet Union.

In 1984 the 'Open Doors' organization began a seven-year campaign to pray for a spiritual turn-around in the Soviet Union, just about the same time as the first hunger strikes by the Chuguyevka community. This prayer offensive in both East and West had come about not because of human organization, but because of the work of the Holy Spirit. What made the Chuguyevka congregation unique was that it had been so alone all these years, utterly without contact with Christians outside the Soviet Union.

But it was unique for another reason. For the first time since the Revolution a congregation was utterly united in its struggles. They did not abandon their prisoners for one moment. They gave the KGB no opportunity to isolate even one of their members. Yet they possessed no clever intellectuals who could outsmart their persecutors. Their only strength was their devotion to each other and their determination to serve only God.

Those long periods of fasting were visible signs of their unity. This powerful weapon moved heaven and earth. They began a seventh hunger strike on 31st March 1987. This time they made a three hundred-day 'relay' fast, with fifty-five adults taking it in turn every two or three days.

The impossible happened: Johan and Ella Vins, their children and grandma Mariya Vins were surprised with a permit to emigrate to West Germany. They arrived in the refugee camp Friedland on 10th April 1987. Shortly afterwards, a cousin invited them to come to Speyer, south of Mannheim.

When they arrived they still felt the effects of the long

journey and they were confused, filled with many questions and concerns. They wondered about Johan's brother who was still a prisoner, along with seven other brothers. They also wondered what was happening to the others in Chuguyevka.

What did God intend by this separation? Had it been an administrative error, or was it the result of Johan's success in penetrating the US embassy? Or did the KGB think that he would forget his brothers and sisters? The first few weeks they felt disoriented. What could they do on behalf of the congregation? They still fasted, but was that the limit of their service?

The truth is, that if the KGB had realized Johan's gifts, they would have revoked their decision immediately. Johan, and even more his mother, spoke the best German of all the congregation. Moreover, they were good communicators, a gift so very few Soviet Union citizens possessed before *glasnost*.

After Johan made contact with Western Christians, Keston College and 'Open Doors' printed a special newsletter that contained the complete story of the Chuguyevka Christians. This *Chuguyevka Pravda* was distributed throughout the West, and thus *pravda* ('truth') was brought to light about that unknown area, far from Moscow.

Without widespread knowledge of this situation, the KGB of Chuguyevka might have continued their persecution of Christians for a longer period. But this *pravda* caused thousands of Christians to begin specific prayers for the Chuguyevka Christians. Abundant proof arrived in the form of the thousands of cards with Bible texts and words of encouragement that both prisoners and church members received from the West. The struggles weren't over yet, but the end was in sight.

In June 1987 Olga Vins received permission to leave with

her eight children. it was a difficult moment for all. Should she leave Nikolai behind in prison? Yet all the prisoners, including Nikolai, had made it known that everyone who received a permit, should go, even the wives of prisoners. They were convinced that every eye-witness from Chuguyevka who could communicate with the West would bring freedom one step closer.

Olga departed with mixed feelings. She dreaded the long journey to that unknown Germany, through nine time zones. Most of the journey was by air, and they arrived at Frankfurt airport on 27th June. Johan, Ella and the others were waiting for them. First Olga and her family had to go to the refuge camp for the required registrations, but they ended up in a flat in the same neighbourhood as Johan.

Frida Walter, Viktor's mother, had left at about the same time, not to the West, but to Arkhangelsk. She too had received an exit visa, but her emigration had been delayed at the last moment. But now that she had a passport, this courageous widow dared to make the trip of about five thousand miles to the Matygori camp, accompanied by her youngest son Pavel. Together they walked the long lonely road. At the entrance they were stopped by an officer who told them they had no permission to enter.

'Of course not', Frida said. 'My son has been here for almost two years and he has never had permission for visitors. Those are your rules. But you ought to be ashamed of yourself. I simply won't leave without seeing him.'

The officer left, and then returned with another one. Frida wouldn't change her mind and she managed to get permission to talk with Viktor via a telephone from behind a glass wall. This was the first time since his departure from the Vladivostok prison that Viktor had seen his mother and brother. He was weak, and spoke so softly that sometimes they could hardly hear him. Frida was startled by his appearance. He was only thirty-seven but his short hair was completely grey. Yet he didn't complain, but inquired after all the members in Chuguyevka.

After two hours the visit was rudely terminated. Frida couldn't leave behind any of the gifts for Viktor. But she confronted the guards and said, 'Do you think that I've travelled a full week for only two hours of talk with my son? Do you think I'm going to take my gifts home again? You're wrong! You'll have to drag me away from here, and the whole world will hear about it. You give me normal family visiting privileges, one or two days, and without this glass partition.' The guards were taken aback by this courageous old woman. They telephoned a highly-placed KGB man, and when he arrived a few hours later, he gave permission for a longer visit. 'Come back tomorrow, and you'll have a room for both of you and prisoner Viktor Walter.'

And that's what happened. The KGB needed the day to install a listening bug, but Frida got her way. Viktor was proud of his mother, who had lost nothing of her spunk. They talked continuously for two days. Viktor already knew of the emigration of Johan and Ella, and Olga after them. 'It's terrific that Olga went', Viktor said. 'Nikolai will feel good about that, I'm sure.'

He was right. The news reached Nikolai via a letter. Shortly afterwards he was summoned by the KGB, who had read the letter first, of course. Nikolai didn't even let the KGB official begin. 'I trust you understand, we've won! My brother, my wife and children, they are all in Germany, and you can do with me whatever you want. My life isn't that important. We've won. The whole congregation will be in Germany before long.'

But the KGB officer ignored Nikolai's challenging words and picked a document off the desk. 'Here,' he said, 'something from Moscow. We have to release you, but we'll interpret that to mean that you may work outside the camp.

We'll tell you where, and you'll have to return each night.'

But Nikolai wasn't much concerned with what they would do with him, for his major concern was the safety of his dear Olga and their children.

In 1987 Russia was full of news about freedom for prisoners. Famous dissidents and Christians were led from camps directly to planes that flew them to the West. Others were allowed to go home. Even so, little hope was raised for the eight Chuguyevka prisoners as yet. Nikolai Vins, Bernhard Rosher and Viktor Samsonov, all three captive in Central Asia, were only put to work outside the labour camp.

It used to be that such a lighter punishment was evidence of prisoners having given in to the KGB. Now the KGB used it to sow possible suspicion about these three among their Chuguyevka friends. But those brothers and sisters trusted each other without reserve. Viktor Walter was also offered a lighter punishment, but he always refused. He said, 'I'm the pastor of the congregation. Those others are prisoners because they protested at my arrest, so I can't accept any reduction in my punishment unless all the others are released.'

Unrest spread in the Gulag Archipelago. Rumours about thousands of prisoners about to be freed made both prisoners and guards nervous. Yet the effect on the Chuguyevka eight was limited to labour camp transfers.

Viktor Walter's camp was closed on 15th December, 1987 and all prisoners were transferred to another one, about twenty miles away. The Dzhanga camp of Nikolai Vins closed around the turn of the year. He was put on transport to Khabarovsk, north of Chuguyevka. During the two months it took him to get there, his family, now in Germany, knew nothing about him. As mentioned before, Tolya Sheludkov had been put in a hospital by the end of 1987.

Beginning in October 1987, families departed for Germany on a regular basis. The Primorski KGB kept losing ground. The depressing clouds began to evaporate and the rest of the population extended more and more sympathy to them. People who hadn't dared even to greet them before, now dropped in for a chat. The neighbours with criminal records who had caused them so much grief, confessed their sins and told them how the KGB had blackmailed them, by promising amnesty from their remaining sentence if they did what the KGB told them to.

Yet the Chuguyevka Christians in both Germany and the Soviet Union did not see any change in the treatment of their beloved prisoners. They agreed to launch a simultaneous demonstration in both Bonn and Moscow on 18th January 1988. The church members still in Chuguyevka drafted a joint letter to the First Party Secretary of the Province of Primorski, announcing that they would demonstrate if the prisoners had not been released by 10th January.

When nothing happened by that date, Vladimir Walter, Anatolia Khokha, Valeri Lobsov, Pavel Betcher and Viktor Betcher travelled to Moscow. In spite of the increased number of inspections along the route because of their letter, they managed to reach the appropriate government building in Moscow without interception. At 10 o'clock on the morning of 18th January they unfurled their banners close to the entrance, with a previously tipped off American television crew busily recording their peaceful demonstration.

The banners read: 'Allow us to leave the Soviet Union', 'We want to leave for West Germany' and 'Free the eight innocent prisoners from the pentecostal congregation in Chuguyevka.'

After about twenty minutes, and with the TV crew gone, the police arrested them all. From their station the police rang Chuguyevka, where no one was aware that these five pentecostals were in Moscow. 'You'll pay for this', the Moscow KGB functionary barked over the phone. The same man asked the five about their further plans. Vladimir told him that he wanted a discussion with Kharchev, the head of religious affairs. After a full day of interrogation, they were released at 7 p.m. on condition that they left Moscow within three days. Their appointment with Kharchev was to take place the next day. As soon as they were free again, they telephoned Johan Vins in Germany. The demonstration in Bonn had also been a success. Their case had gained the attention of many politicians, and even Sheverdnadze, the Russian Foreign secretary who was visiting Bonn at the time, had taken notice of their presence. As it turned out, these two demonstrations resulted in a number of releases in the spring of 1988.

The sentence of Viktor Samsonov was finished on 27th December 1987. No one heard anything about him, until he suddenly appeared in Chuguyevka at the end of January 1988. The first prisoner had returned.

Shortly after this they were surprised by the sudden release of Oleg Lobanov, the young Christian who had recorded all the KGB crimes on film. Officially he still had seven months to go. In February 1988 he saw his wife Olga and two children again. Samuel, named after Samuel Walter, had been born shortly before his arrest in 1985. He was a toddler now, three years old, who only knew his father from a picture.

In the spring of 1988 the day really dawned for the Chuguyevka congregation. Bernhard Rosher returned on 25th April. Three days later Peter Walter was summoned to appear before his camp commandant. He was asked to sit down and told that the rest of his sentence had been remitted. They even gave him a train ticket home. But Peter had an intuition that he'd better not take too much time travelling, so with his last money he managed to buy a plane ticket to Khabarovsk and from there he took the train to Chuguyevka. He never even had time to warn anybody. As he walked down Beregovaya Street, his heart beat faster and faster. He saw Lyudmila Teplikh, the community's nurse. 'Lyuba', he called from a distance. She looked up, ready to answer back, but then she clamped her hand to her mouth. Peter walked on and saw that she couldn't believe her eyes, for his sentence was not supposed to be finished until the end of the year. But then she recognized him and ran to Anna, Peter's wife, to tell her the news.

That day Chuguyevka had a party, and Speyer had one too after it received a telegram. Peter's quick trip by air had been a good thing, for Anna had received a visa for Germany and she left a few days later. Peter stayed behind for now, waiting for all the other prisoners to be released.

The next surprise took another three weeks. Tolya Sheludkov was freed. Seriously ill, he arrived on 20th May. He had been forced to take medicines meant only for mentally ill patients. Tolya needed to get his strength back, with the loving help of Olga and all the other church members. They had an additional problem. These two were not of German descent, and their emigration would be more difficult. But they also had this consolation: Viktor Walter and the others would not abandon them in Chuguyevka.

Vladimir Walter had also emigrated to Germany, and he led a growing congregation that now numbered a hundred and forty men, women and children. A number of families lived for a while in a refuge camp close to Worms. Viktor Walter's wife, Mariya, also emigrated with her seven children. Being a Russian, she had to remain in two small rooms in Speyer until her husband could come, for only then would she be treated as German herself.

25
A Wearisome Ending

Yegor Betcher was given the responsibility of looking after the few who remained in Chuguyevka, and he would stay until all the prisoners were released. The major struggle now focused on Viktor Pavlovets in the labour camp close to Chuguyevka.

Nikolai Vins was still a prisoner in Khabarovsk, the camp he'd been taken to after the closing of the one close to the Caspian Sea. He now enjoyed a small measure of freedom and was able to telephone his wife in Germany once in a while. Yet he had to finish his sentence in Khabarovsk and report to the labour camp each evening.

Viktor Walter could have been released already, but he refused unless the other two were released first. In April he was brought from Arkhangelsk to the Chuguyevka camp, where he arrived on 4th May, now behind the same barbed wire as Viktor even though they were still forcibly separated.

The congregation, now in two places, was confused about KGB intentions. Within a few days it became clear that the transfer of their pastor wasn't all that positive a move. Perhaps the local KGB saw it as an opportunity for inflicting a last measure of suffering. On entering the camp his Bible was confiscated. He had managed to retain this treasure thus far, but in the Chuguyevk camp even that was taken away.

Of course Viktor Walter looked for any opportunity to talk to Viktor Pavlovets. They spotted each other in the shower hall a few days after Walter's arrival, but had no chance to talk. They belonged to different camp groupings, and conversations between groups were strictly prohibited.

On 12th May Viktor Pavlovets found himself peeling potatoes in the camp kitchen which was located next to the recreation hall. A film was shown that afternoon, and through the window he saw Viktor Walter entering as part of a group. He managed to leave the kitchen unnoticed, slip into the hall and seat himself in one of the back rows. When his eyes got used to the dark, he looked around for his pastor. But before he could spot him, his arm was grabbed by an officer, who dragged him out of the hall and told him: 'Why are you here, Pavlovets? I know, you're trying to locate prisoner Walter. I consider your attempt equal to having succeeded: twelve days in solitary.'

Poor Viktor was used to being locked up for the slightest infraction, but when Viktor Walter heard what they had done to his friend he used every opportunity to protest. As far as the prison authorities and especially Major Grigori Gevashelishvili were concerned, however, Viktor Pavlovets could perish for all they cared. The Chuguyevka KGB was under some Moscow pressure, for news about cruelties in this eastern province had spread widely by now. After eight days Viktor Pavlovets was suddenly taken out of his cell and secretly transported to Vladivostok by Black Raven. Viktor thought he was merely being transferred to another camp.

In the Vladivostok gaol they told them that he needed another operation. The surgeon asked what ailed him. 'I've got a lot wrong with me, but I have never asked for an operation. All I know is that the last one made things a lot worse.'

'Well, would they send you here for nothing?' the surgeon asked, to which Viktor replied, 'I have no idea why I'm here. Probably an administrative error.' But a few days later it was clear that the KGB had not made an administrative error, for they insisted that Viktor's former operation be repeated. Was he on his way to freedom? Why this sudden concern about a failed operation? Viktor had heard that sometimes dissidents were 'repaired' before they departed for the West. On 3rd June he returned to the Chuguyevka camp, feeling much better.

Bykov, the head of the KGB, visited Viktor Walter, who still didn't know what had happened to his young friend. Bykov told him about the operation and said, 'You see, we treated your stubborn friend very well. Now it's your turn to disappear to Germany. Moscow has given orders to release you and see to it that you're in Germany within two weeks.'

'You'll have to release Viktor Pavlovets and Nikolai Vins first', Viktor Walter replied without a smile. Bykov shook his head and departed.

The Georgian major who had made a sport out of harassing Viktor Pavlovets now turned his attention to Viktor Walter. He spread rumours that prisoner Walter was a dangerous Nazi, making clever use of the old 'Red Banner' story about Viktor's uncle who was supposed to have been a torturer in a German concentration camp. A few prisoners believed the story, and Viktor had to be constantly on guard against retaliations.

He decided to write the following letter to the supreme officer of justice in the Soviet Union:

'In the labour camp of Chuguyevka, my fellow prisoner Viktor Pavlovets and I, kept here only because of our faith, are constantly under threat of death. Major Gevashelishvili is doing everything in his power to abuse us. I would request of you to transfer us to the Vladivostok prison, get us into solitary, or put a stop to these cruel crimes against us.'

Lieutenant Colonel Bykov soon appeared. He told Viktor

Walter, 'Go on, complain about the camp authorities, but you could already have been in Germany with your wife and children.' Viktor simply said: 'Don't waste time coming with the same proposals.'

Bykov knew he had lost, and more to himself than to Viktor he said, 'You'll get your way again. In all these years you've never done what we wanted you to.' With a tired look on his face he looked at his prisoner and said, 'OK, we'll release Pavlovets and then you can go to Germany together." Not yet, not before Nikolai Vins is free too. Not one member of our congregation will be left behind.'

The next day – 11th July 1988 – Viktor Walter worked at his job as usual, but when he returned at 6 p.m., he was separated from his fellow prisoners. He wasn't allowed back into the barracks and had to go to the camp offices. There he heard that he was to leave the camp forthwith, and that his friends were already on their way to get him. He didn't even have time to say goodbye to the other prisoners. Soon he stood outside the gate, where Yegor Betcher and his brother Peter were waiting for him. Viktor Walter was free indeed, but Viktor Pavlovets was still inside the camp. Had Bykov outfoxed him after all?

The news spread quickly, first over the camp, then in Primorski, and in Germany, and finally over the whole world. The authorities even provided a brief furlough for Nikolai Vins to meet with his friend and pastor, although he had to report back to the Khabarovsk camp afterwards.

After another month Tolya Sheludkov and Bernhard Rosher left for Germany with their families. That left only about twenty church members in Chuguyevka, with about a hundred and seventy-five now living in and around the city of Worms in West Germany.

Viktor Walter and the others worked feverishly for the release of Viktor Pavlovets. Constantly they reminded the government of its own promises to release him. Finally, two months after the release of Viktor Walter, the great day dawned. On 13th September Viktor Walter received assurance that Viktor Pavlovets would be released the next day. They departed for the camp immediately. When they shouted the information across the barriers, it was news to their brother.

The morning of the 14th began normally, with his 7 a.m. shift in the factory. He had a sense of expectation about what might happen that day, but when a guard took him away at 10 a.m., he was still surprised. He was taken to the same room where he had been interrogated so often. A judge, a prosecutor and the officer in command of his prison section were waiting for him.

'Have you been sentenced lately?' the judge asked. Viktor told him all the details of the previous year. The judge already knew it all from the list in front of him. With that many 'transgressions' a longer sentence could easily have been manufactured, but the judge created a new document that showed no misdemeanours for a full year previously. This way the judicial system could not prevent his release, and the Kremlin's wishes could be attended to. Viktor realized how these manoeuvres were meant to protect their own position.

By the end of this secret session Viktor heard that he was acquitted, without any acknowledgement that he had been convicted without due cause, and had spent over three hundred days in solitary confinement. But he was tired of the lies, and left without saying a word to this court of justice. Major Grigori, the one who had made his life so miserable, was angry and said, 'We don't even treat prisoners who collaborate with us this favourably'. But even he couldn't hold this hated Chuguyevka Christian any longer.

The news of his release spread like wildfire through the camp. Whoever had an opportunity, said goodbye. Viktor didn't have to work the next day, and on 16th September, shortly after lunch, the gate swung open for him. He waved to the other prisoners and they motioned to him to turn around. There the old Volga approached, with Viktor Walter as driver. They embraced for the first time in many years, and many tears flowed. Both Viktors drove slowly past the fence and waved until they could no longer see anyone.

At 7 o'clock the next morning Viktor Pavlovets came back for one more camp appointment. As per custom, a freed prisoner returned for a final 'gift' to the friends who remained behind. He knew where he could throw the parcel, for the weak spots in camp protection were well known by now. The food parcel, containing tea, sausages, sweets, milk, cheese and other valuables, safely reached its destination, as a voice from behind the barrier testified. He left the camp for good, not without some pain, for as he had suffered there, so he had made many friends. Would he ever see them again?

Nikolai Vins was finally released on 22nd October 1988. There could be only one explanation for the long delay: the East Siberian authorities wanted to pretend it was their decision, even if they knew they had lost the battle long ago.

The brothers organized a last tour of the five sister congregations, celebrating communion and blessing the elders who had shown their dedication and trustworthiness over so many years. Christians from these small congregations had supported the Chuguyevka congregation so strongly in all this time. Now the mission work would fall on them. A foundation had been laid, but Primorski still counted many corners where the Gospel had not yet been heard.

Viktor Walter had to go to Vladivostok on emigration business. There he met Bykov again, the KGB chief who had been personally responsible for the persecution. His attitude had turned around completely. He no longer spoke as an enemy, but as someone who found it hard to say goodbye to his victims because his own life had lost meaning.

He stuck out his hand and said, 'Dear Viktor, how nice it would be if we could have a conversation after all these years.' Viktor didn't forget for one moment that he was still in the Soviet Union. Determined, yet kindly, he said, 'Before you say something, Mr Bykov, I want to ask you this: if we have done something wrong, and if you still blame us for that, then we want to ask you for forgiveness. Under no circumstances do we want to go away from here leaving unconfessed sins behind.'

Bykov put both his hands to his face. 'Oh no, certainly not! We at the KGB consider both you and your congregation examples of one great miracle. I'll tell you why. You are the first Christians since the 1917 October Revolution who have made our Soviet government back down. Do you realize that? Our important Moscow leaders have taken a step back in the face of your small band here in Chuguyevka. The very first time in history. You won! We respect you for it. Like genuine heroes, you have maintained your objectives. When it comes to persistence, you've proved yourselves to be our equal. And I think we've been wrong. We thought we could break you as we did other Christians, but for the first time we have not succeeded.'

Viktor could hardly believe his ears. After so many years of hatred and brutal violence, it was difficult to understand such a turn-around. He replied, 'What would you have done in our shoes?' Bykov thought for a moment and then answered, slowly, 'I don't know. Possibly the same thing.'

'Mr Bykov,' Viktor said, 'you seem to acknowledge that we were not anti-Soviet, but simple people who wanted to obey God. And that we had the right to defend the interests of our children.'

'Of course', the man said. 'We came to understand that and that's why we are now letting you depart in peace. Just make a list of all the people you want to take with you to Germany.'

His generosity came very late, but Viktor still had enough items on his list of wishes. Tolya Sheludkov had two sisters in Chuguyevka, and he knew of some other Russians who were loosely connected to the congregation. He wrote down their names and gave the list to Bykov. 'These people belong with us. I hold you to your word and we'll see them in Germany too.'

They said goodbye, this pastor of the Chuguyevka church and the leader of more than six years of persecution.

Their houses had been sold and most of their other possessions, such as furniture, cars and motorcycles, had been given to the evangelists in their sister congregations.

On 7th November 1988, the plane with the last load of Chuguyevka Christians arrived at the airport at Frankfurt-am-Main. The reunion of Viktor and Nikolai with their families was most moving. A choir sang in the reception hall and many new Western friends had joined the entire congregation.

A new life

After the new arrivals had spent a few days in the refugee camp, the congregation was together again. They received a beautiful piece of land to build eighteen new houses plus a church in Guntersblum, a lovely village on the Rhine. From now on the congregation would be called the *Freie Evangeliums-christen-Gemeinde Guntersblum*. A new era had begun; a new life. It would present its own unique challenges to the community.

Life in West Germany was so different: less black and

white, and also less hostile. Yet spiritually it had its own unique threats. It's not so easy to switch from total isolation to a life lived in the middle of diverse opinions.

In the Soviet Union their community had been a clearly visible alternative, in which each member had to make choices in each new situation. Community living held many advantages. But in the West it is far easier and more convenient, often less costly too, to have each family live by itself. Two of the families soon chose the more individualistic lifestyle of the West, and it didn't surprise anyone. While the separation was painful after so many years of joint resistance, the community's mood remained realistic.

Here is how Viktor Walter sees the new situation.

'We have much to learn yet about our new purpose. We don't simply want to hang on to our lifestyle. We only want to hang on to the Word of God, love for each other, and to our task of being a light for other human beings God places in our way. Sanctification through suffering is not only a matter of our past. We're still walking "the narrow way".

'The snares set for the Church of Christ in the West are perhaps more difficult to detect than the roaring of atheist lions.

'James begins his epistle with these words, valid now as for the times when we still lived in the Soviet Union:

'Consider it pure joy, my brothers, whenever you face trials of many kinds, because you know that the testing of your faith develops perseverance. Perseverance must finish its work so that you may be mature and complete, not lacking anything.'

If you would like to receive further information about "Open Doors with Brother Andrew" and its ministry to the Suffering Church worldwide, please write to us.

Upon your request we gladly send you — free of charge — our monthly magazine, which gives up-to-date news, information and prayer items about persecuted Christians around the world.

Name..

Address...

....

Postal Code..

Place...

Country..

Forward this form to the office nearest you.

Open Doors	Open Doors	Open Doors
P.O. Box 6	Box 27001	P.O. Box 53
Witney	Santa Ana	Seaforth
Oxon	CA 92799	NSW 2092
OX8 7SP	USA	Australia
England		

Open Doors International — Headquarters
P.O. Box 47
3840 AA Harderwijk
Holland